THE WORLD OF SCIENCE
PROJECTS

THE WORLD OF SCIENCE
PROJECTS

RON TAYLOR

Facts On File Publications
New York, New York • Bicester, England

PROJECTS

Copyright © Macdonald & Co. (Publishers) Ltd. 1986

First published in the United States of America in 1986
by Facts on File, Inc., 460 Park Avenue South, New
York, N.Y. 10016

First published in Great Britain in 1986 by
Orbis Book Publishing Corporation Limited, London
A member of Maxwell Pergamon Publishing Corporation plc

Library of Congress Cataloging in Publication Data

Main entry under title:

World of Science

  Includes index.
Summary; A twenty-five volume encyclopedia of
scientific subjects, designed for eight-to twelve-year-olds.
One volume is entirely devoted to projects.
  1. Science—Dictionaries, Juvenile.   Science—
Dictionaries
Q121.J86   1984   500   84-1654

ISBN: 0-8160-1076-5

Printed in Italy
10 9 8 7 6 5 4 3 2

Consultant editors
Eleanor Felder, Former Managing Editor, **New Book of
Knowledge** James Neujahr, Dean of the School of
Education, City College of New York
Ethan Signer, Professor of Biology, Massachusetts
Institute of Technology
J. Tuzo Wilson, Director General, Ontario Science Centre

Previous pages
Plants take time to
become established and
grow to the size of the
ones in and around
this garden pond. But
be patient and the
plants you grow by
your pond (pages 52–
53) will be as fine as
these in a year or two.

Editor Penny Clarke
Designer Roger Kohn

Note There are some unusual words in this book. They are explained in the Glossary on pages 62–63. The first time each word is used in the text it is printed in *italics*.

▲More a flying toy than a hunting weapon, the boomerang was invented thousands of years ago in Australia. More things to make and fly are described on page 44.

PUZZLES, CODES AND COMPUTERS

SOME SCIENCE PUZZLES

To many people, science is just one big puzzle. Such people are often at a disadvantage today, when many of the more go-ahead jobs and professions demand a working knowledge of at least one branch of science. Because learning science often *can* be difficult, modern textbooks of elementary science sometimes include science puzzles such as the ones shown on this page. Solving such puzzles is an entertaining way of learning the basic principles of a difficult branch of science such as *physics*. Once you know these basic principles, you can go on to solve other science problems all the more easily.

▶A rope passes around a pulley and is attached at one end to a weight exactly equal to that of a man, who then starts to climb the rope. Does the weight sink down as he climbs, so pulling him up on to the pulley? If not, what does happen?

▼A van is carrying a load of birds. Its shaking disturbs the birds into flight. Does this make the van's load less and so save fuel?

▶A supertechnology drill is used to bore a hole right through the Earth. Someone then drops a stone down the hole. Does the stone travel right through the Earth and come out the other side? (Assume that the Earth is a perfect sphere.)

◀What has yoga to do with science puzzles? Well, yogis manage to balance in surprising ways, and to do this it helps to have a scientific knowledge of the body.

▶If a train is going north, some points on the train are travelling south. How? Cut out a large circle and another smaller one in thick cardoard or rigid polystyrene foam. Stick the smaller one in the middle of the larger. Make a hole through the larger piece and glue in a short pencil as shown. Pin a sheet of drawing paper to the wall and put a wooden rail – or the edge of a table – just in front. Roll the wheel on its flange along the rail so that the pencil draws a curve on the paper. The result (**right**) shows that the lowest points on the curve travel in the opposite direction to the wheel. The curve shown here is called a curtate cycloid. You can draw other kinds of cycloid by glueing the pencil nearer the centre of the wheel.

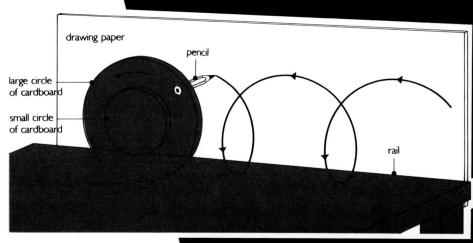

drawing paper

large circle of cardboard

small circle of cardboard

pencil

rail

▲Holography makes images of a subject which are not flat like a photograph, but are 3-dimensional, having depth in space. A laser beam is first used to make a hologram of the subject, then a second laser beam is shone on the hologram to create the 3-dimensional image.

a No. The extra air pressure downwards when the birds are in flight exactly balances their weight when on the van floor, so the load remains the same.
b The man on one side of the pulley exactly balances the weight on the other side, so as he climbs, the weight rises.
c No. The stone falls into the Earth at increasing speed because of the Earth's gravity. This is greatest at the centre. The stone shoots past the centre but then starts to slow down because gravity is pulling it the other way. By the time it reaches the opposite surface of the Earth, it has slowed down completely. Then it starts to fall again towards the Earth's centre – and so on, if not for ever, then for a very long time indeed!

After speech, drawing and writing are the most familiar ways in which we communicate with one another. The discovery of each was a milestone in our 3-million-years-long history. The earliest people first learned to speak perhaps about 100,000 years ago. The first human drawings and paintings came much later – the earliest found so far are about 30,000 years old. Writing was invented later still, by the Sumerians in *Mesopotamia* about 5,000 years ago. Now we have a multitude of different alphabets, and many ways of producing or reproducing words and pictures. Here are a few more...

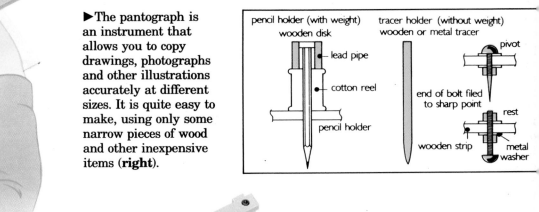

pencil holder (with weight)
wooden disk
– lead pipe
– cotton reel
pencil holder

tracer holder (without weight)
wooden or metal tracer
pivot
end of bolt filed to sharp point
rest
wooden strip
metal washer

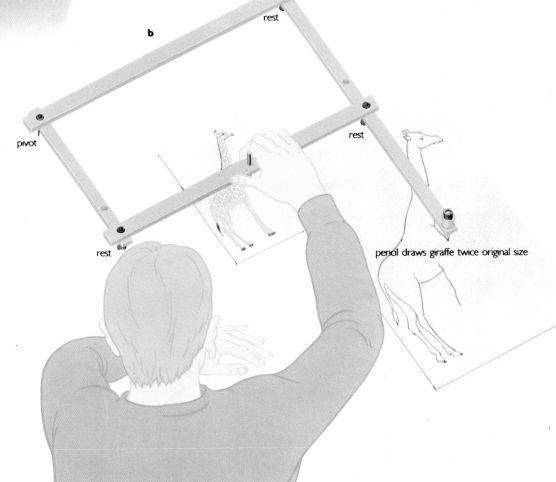

a
20 cm (8 in)
pivot
rest
40 cm (16 in)
pencil holder
wooden strip
20 cm (8 in)
pencil draws map half original size
rest
tracer moved over outline of map
rest

▶The pantograph is an instrument that allows you to copy drawings, photographs and other illustrations accurately at different sizes. It is quite easy to make, using only some narrow pieces of wood and other inexpensive items (**right**).

▲With the pencil and the tracer in the positions shown, you can use the pantograph to copy an illustration such as a map at half its original size.

▶Exchange the positions of pencil, tracer and lead weight, and you can copy an illustration, this time at double its original size. If you hold the pantograph lightly but firmly at the pivot point, it won't slide while you're making the copy.

rest
b
pivot
rest
rest
pencil draws giraffe twice original size

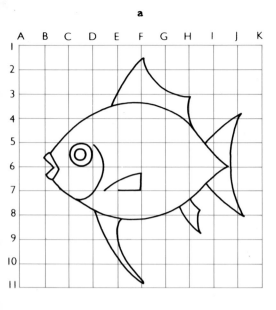
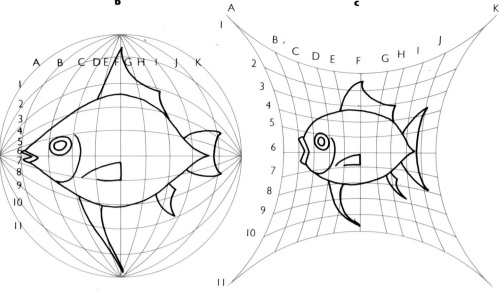

a

A B C D E F G H I J K
1 2 3 4 5 6 7 8 9 10 11

b

A B C D E F G H I J K
1 2 3 4 5 6 7 8 9 10 11

c

A B C D E F G H I J K
1 2 3 4 5 6 7 8 9 10 11

▲Exact distortions

Draw or trace a shape, eg a fish, onto a sheet of ordinary graph paper. Letter and number the horizontal and vertical lines as shown. Then transfer the drawing on to ruled paper with a different grid, but with the same letter/number code. For example, start at B5, the upper part of the fish's mouth, and then carry on through several other points, E3, J4... etc, until the whole shape is copied. The two distortion graphs here have curved grids, but you can also use graphs with slanting or straight line grids, wavy grids or mixed straight and curved grids.

This is a mirror message!

mirror

paper

message! This is a mirror

◄You can use mirror writing for secret messages. For example, you can write your diary using it so that others can't easily read it, without a mirror handy.

◄Numerals through the ages and across the world. The first writing, including numbers, was made in Mesopotamia, on clay tablets, such as the one **below**.

Sumerian-Babylonian										
Ancient Egyptian	I	II	III	IIII						∩
Mayan		•	••	•••	••••	—				
Ancient Greek	A	B	Γ	Δ	E	F	Z	H	Θ	I
Chinese	一	二	三	四	五	六	七	八	九	十
Roman	I	II	III	IV	V	VI	VII	VIII	IX	X
Hindu	0	1	2	3	4	5	6	7	8	9
Arabic	•	1	2	3	4	5	6	7	8	9
Modern	0	1	2	3	4	5	6	7	8	9	10

How the abacus shows numbers

An abacus (**below**) can show numbers up to 9,999,999,999. Two smaller numbers are shown **far right**: 672 and 2,829. To add move beads down the wires. To take away (subtract) move beads up the wires.

BUILD A COMPUTER

We think of computers as complicated electronic machines, invented in the last 40 years or so. In fact, computers have been around since ancient times, in the form of the abacus, a simple calculating machine still used widely in many parts of the world. Calculating with the abacus means moving beads about on wires. Some of the calculations, especially multiplication and division, may seem long-winded and laborious, but practice makes perfect, and it is possible, sometimes, for someone using an abacus to beat someone using a microcomputer!

Make the abacus frame to the size you want from hardwood 2.4 cm (1 in) square. Drill holes into long sides of frame to take the wires. Insert wires and glue in place

Secure frame's joints with wood glue and screw

10 metal wires: use stiff coathanger wire bent into a slight curve or arc to prevent beads slipping down during a calculation

10 large beads on each wire. The beads can be of any material, but the column should come to just below halfway up the wire

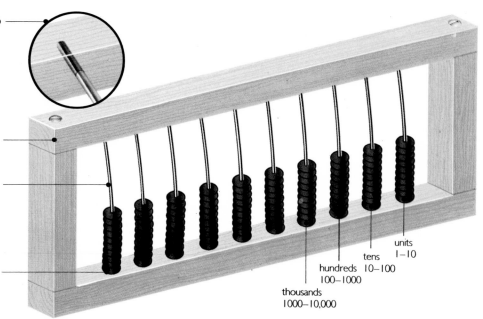

thousands 1000–10,000

hundreds 10–100 100–1000

tens 10–100

units 1–10

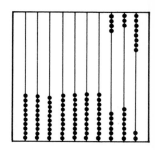

▲The figure 672 set out on the abacus.

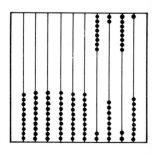

▲The figure 2,829 as it is shown on the abacus.

Addition:
754 + 83

1 Set the number 754 on the last three wires – the hundreds, tens and units wires

2 Add (move down) 3 beads on the units wire

3 Try to add 8 beads to the tens wire. This would make 13 beads, so instead add 3 beads to the tens wire and 1 bead (carried over) to the hundreds wire
Answer: 837

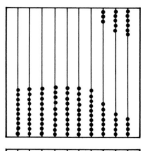

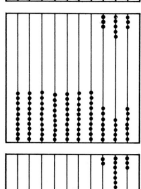

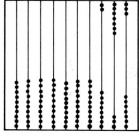

Subtraction:
1027 – 321

1 Set 1027 on the abacus wires

2 Take away (move up) 1 bead on the units wire. Take away 2 beads on the tens wire
3 Look at the hundreds wire. You cannot take away three beads on it because it reads zero. So take away (or 'borrow') one bead from the next wire up, the thousands wire. This gives you 10 hundreds to take away from. You need take away only 3 hundreds, so move 7 beads down on the hundreds wire.
Answer: 706

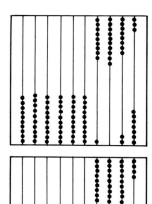

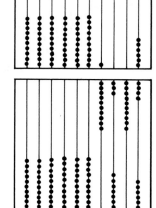

Multiplying:
Multiplying is repeated addition. Example: $9 \times 3 = 9 + 9 + 9$ or 9 three times. $27 \times 13 = 27$ added to itself 13 times. How quickly can you do this on your abacus?

Dividing:
Dividing is repeated subtraction. Example: $360 \div 24$. Set up 360 on the abacus, then take away 24. Then take away another 24, then another, and so on. When you have repeated this 15 times the abacus reads zero, so the answer is 15

▲Restaurants can be busy places. This one in the Far East is no exception, with dozens of customers waiting to be served, each with half-a-dozen or more different dishes. Adding up the costs of all these variously-priced dishes is a tricky business, even for the practised operator of an abacus.

◄Microcomputers are the latest and most sophisticated tools of science and business. In the photograph, the operator has asked the microcomputer to print out some results on the monitor by typing the instruction on the keyboard.

MAGIC SQUARES

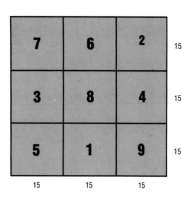

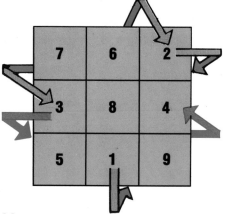

► As you can see, this grid works, so try the puzzle with a grid of 5 squares across and down and enter the numbers 1–25. Puzzled? The diagram shows you how to get the answer right without a computer!

◄ Start with 1 in the middle square of the bottom row. To know where to put the next number (always enter them in sequence) *move one square down and to the right.* Follow the arrows when you can't do that. If a square is full move to the left. Yes, if you follow the arrow 4 *is* on the left of 3!

▼ The Aztecs of Mexico made this stone calendar, on which their Sun god, Tonatiuh, is surrounded by signs and symbols including those for the days of the Aztec year. The calendar stone was used, among other things, for the computation or calculation of eclipses of the Sun.

The magic square is a very old mathematical puzzle, but it still makes a good game to try out on your computer. In the days before computers, you drew up a grid of squares and put a number in each square. You could only use whole numbers (1, 2, 3 etc), you could not repeat a number, or use nought. The object of the game was to make each row and column of figures add up to the same total. The grids of three squares (above) are really quite easy, but with a computer you can have fun making much more complicated ones.

Remember that the grid must consist of an odd number of squares, and that you can only use whole numbers, no noughts and no repeated numbers.

▼ The bigger the magic square you want to make the longer it'll take to do. But this program produced the squares at the top of the next page. It is written in Microsoft BASIC, so it is suitable for most home computers. Check the manual of yours if you're not sure if it will need adapting or not. The program asks for the number of rows (and therefore the columns) in the magic square, then checks that this is a whole, odd number. At line 90 it starts to compute and display the magic square. Then, from line 250, it checks its own calculations

```
10 REM********************
15 REM***MAGIC SQUARES********
20 REM****SET-UP************
30 M=19:DIM A(M,M)
40 PRINT:PRINT"Magic Squares"
50 PRINT:PRINT"How many rows (1 to 19)";
   :INPUT S
60 IF S<0 OR S<>INT(S) THEN PRINT"ERROR":GOTO
   50
70 IF S>M THEN PRINT"ERROR":GOTO 50
80 IF S/2=INT(S/2) THEN PRINT"ERROR - Odd
Numbers Only":GOTO 50
90 REM**GENERATE SQUARE********
100 X=INT(S/2)+1:Y=S:C=1
110 A(X,Y)=C
120 C=C+1:IF C>S*S THEN GOTO 200
130 X=X+1:IF X>S THEN X=1
140 Y=Y+1:IF Y>S THEN Y=1
150 IF A(X,Y)<>0 THEN X=X-2:Y=Y-1
160 IF Y=0 THEN Y=S
170 IF X=0 THEN X=S
180 IF X=-1 THEN X=S-1
190 GOTO 110
200 REM***PRINT SQUARE*********
210 PRINT:PRINT
220 FOR Y=1 TO S:FOR X=1 TO S
230 A=A(X,Y):GOSUB 380:PRINT" ";A$;" ";
240 NEXT X:PRINT:NEXT Y

250 REM***CHECK ROWS & COLS****
260 F=0
270 FOR Y=1 TO S:T=0
280 FOR X=1 TO S:T=T+A(X,Y):NEXT X
290 IF F=0 THEN U=T:F=1
300 IF T<>U THEN PRINT"ERROR - Row 1 &
Row";Y;" Do Not Match":STOP
310 U=T:NEXT Y
320 FOR X=1 TO S:T=0
330 FOR Y=1 TO S:T=T+A(X,Y):NEXT Y
340 IF T<>U THEN PRINT"ERROR - Row 1 &
Col";X;" Do Not Match":STOP
350 U=T:NEXT X
360 PRINT:PRINT"All rows and cols add to ";T
370 STOP
380 REM****NUM-STRING CONV*****
390 A$=STR$(A)
400 IF LEN(A$)<3 THEN A$=" "+A$:GOTO 400
410 RETURN
```

►This 9 by 9 square was generated by the program bottom right on the opposite page. What does each column and row add up to?

52	42	32	22	12	2	73	72	62
63	53	43	33	23	13	3	74	64
65	55	54	44	34	24	14	4	75
76	66	56	46	45	35	25	15	5
6	77	67	57	47	37	36	26	16
17	7	78	68	58	48	38	28	27
19	18	8	79	69	59	49	39	29
30	20	10	9	80	70	60	50	40
41	31	21	11	1	81	71	61	51

130	114	98	82	66	50	34	18	2	211	210	194	178	162	146
147	131	115	99	83	67	51	35	19	3	212	196	195	179	163
164	148	132	116	100	84	68	52	36	20	4	213	197	181	180
166	165	149	133	117	101	85	69	53	37	21	5	214	198	182
183	167	151	150	134	118	102	86	70	54	38	22	6	215	199
200	184	168	152	136	135	119	103	87	71	55	39	23	7	216
217	201	185	169	153	137	121	120	104	88	72	56	40	24	8
9	218	202	186	170	154	138	122	106	105	89	73	57	41	25
26	10	219	203	187	171	155	139	123	107	91	90	74	58	42
43	27	11	220	204	188	172	156	140	124	108	92	76	75	59
60	44	28	12	221	205	189	173	157	141	125	109	93	77	61
62	46	45	29	13	222	206	190	174	158	142	126	110	94	78
79	63	47	31	30	14	223	207	191	175	159	143	127	111	95
96	80	64	48	32	16	15	224	208	192	176	160	144	128	112
113	97	81	65	49	33	17	1	225	209	193	177	161	145	129

◄An even larger square created by the same type of program (**opposite below right**). Writing programs for a game like this can take quite a while, but the greatest problem is generally the size of your computer's screen. The bigger the square, the longer the individual numbers in the columns, so the greater the room needed on the screen. In general, a 9 by 9 square is likely to be the largest you can produce.

◄An early time calculator – this early English brass clock was made in 1670.

▲A model of an even earlier clock. The original was made in China about 1088.

13

INTELLIGENT ANIMALS

The Animal game opposite is great fun and you can make up similar games using other subjects, your friends, family, countries of the world, school subjects and so on.

The learning trees that such games build up are examples of a program that teaches itself to improve its performance while it is running. At first the program only 'knows' two animals and one question. If it doesn't guess what animal you are thinking about the first time, you have to enter the name of the animal and a question to distinguish it from the animal the program guessed wrongly. This information is added to the program's knowledge to be used next time you play the game. This is called a knowledge-based program.

Data used in this type of program is organized in exactly the same way as in programs devoted to developing artificial intelligence. So though you may run your game on quite a small home computer, it could be 'thinking' along the same lines as a big *mainframe* computer (**below**) or a helpful robot (**left**).

▲Computers of the future may include servant robots that will help about the house.

▶Computers are necessary for the design of spacecraft. The picture **above** shows a microchip, the brain and memory of a computer. This one is greatly magnified.

►This diagram shows the Animals tree after several games have been played. The computer has 'learned' five different animals, with four questions to distinguish between them. From the sample run (red lines), you can see how the computer uses the tree to respond to the player's answers in the next game. This time the player is thinking of a hedgehog and the computer has to learn this new animal when it discovers that the player is not thinking of a lion. The computer then asks for a way to distinguish between a hedgehog and a lion so that it can learn the new animal. Once you've got this far, why not include the camel?

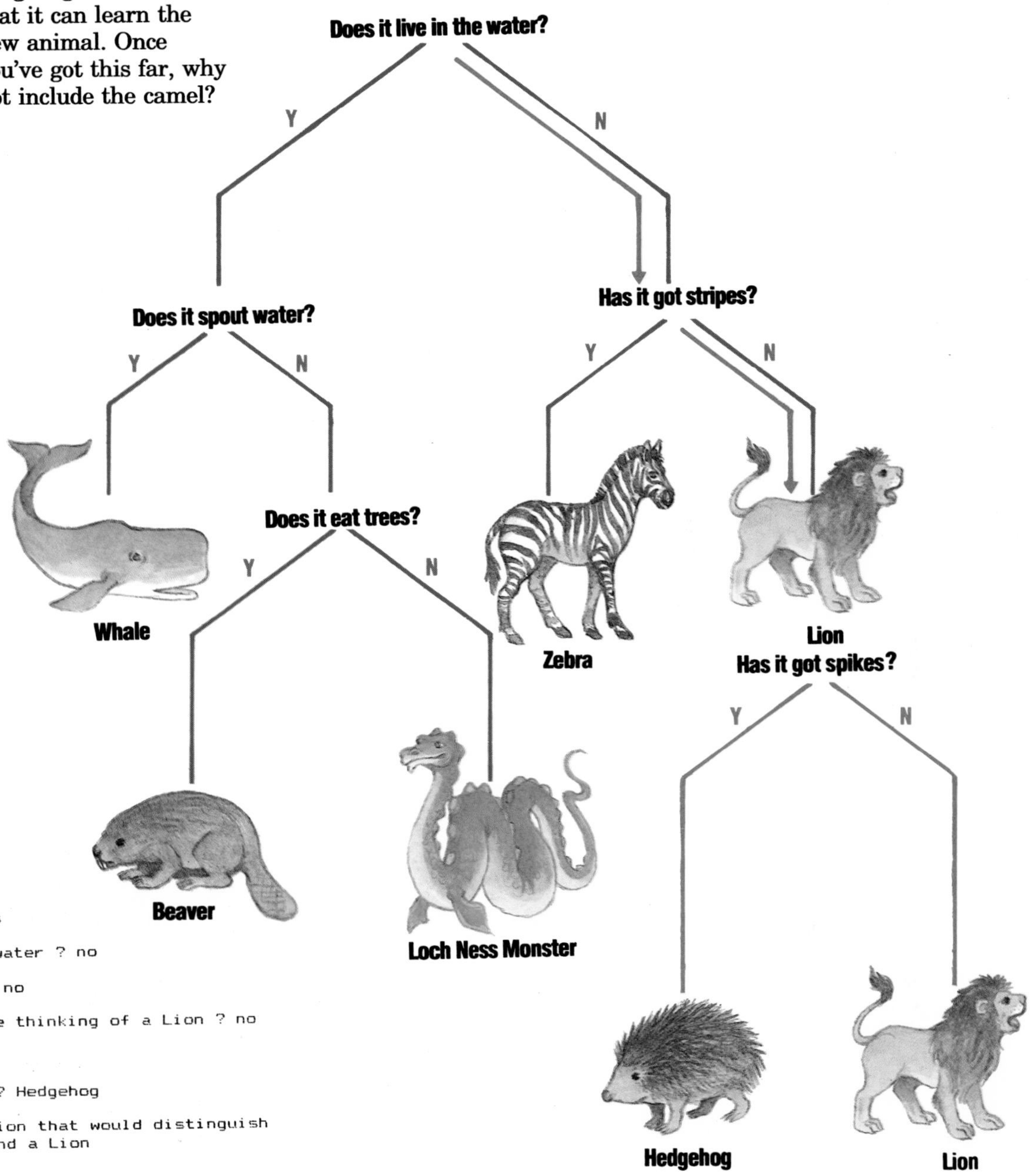

Does it live in the water?

Y   N

Does it spout water?

Y   N

Does it eat trees?

Y   N

Whale

Beaver

Loch Ness Monster

Has it got stripes?

Y   N

Zebra

Lion
Has it got spikes?

Y   N

Hedgehog

Lion

```
Sample Run

Care for a game ? yes

Does it live in the water ? no

Has it got stripes ? no

Is the animal you are thinking of a Lion ? no

I give up!!!

What is your animal ? Hedgehog

Please enter a question that would distinguish
between a Hedgehog and a Lion
?  Has it got spikes

For a Lion the answer would be ? no

I now know  6  different Animals !

Care for a game ?
```

```
10 REM  Animals game
20 REM
30 REM ** Set up
40 N=100: REM Max no of animals
50 DIM Y(N),N(N),T$(N)
60 C=3:FOR I=1 TO 3:READ Y(I),N(I),T$(I):NEXT I
70 PRINT :PRINT "A N I M A L S !":PRINT
80 GOTO 190
90 REM ** Answer YES or NO
100 PRINT:PRINT Q$;" ";:INPUT A$
110 IF A$="y" OR A$="Y" OR A$="YES" OR A$="yes" THEN A=1:RETURN
120 IF A$="n" OR A$="N" OR A$="NO" OR A$="no" THEN A=0:RETURN
130 PRINT:PRINT"Please answer YES or NO":GOTO 100
140 REM ** Add A or AN to animal name
150 I$=LEFT$(A$,1):P$=" a "
160 IF I$="A" OR I$="E" OR I$="I" OR I$="O" OR I$="U" OR I$="a" OR I$
="e" OR I$="i" OR I$="o" OR I$="u" THEN P$=" an "
170 A$=P$+A$:RETURN
180 REM ** Start a new game
190 Q$="Care for a game":GOSUB 100
200 IF A=0 THEN PRINT:PRINT "BYE!":END
210 P=1
220 REM ** Play game
230 IF Y(P)=0 AND N(P)=0 THEN 290
240 Q$=T$(P):GOSUB 100
250 IF A=1 THEN P=Y(P)
260 IF A=0 THEN P=N(P)
270 GOTO 230
280 REM ** Make a guess at the animal
290 A$=T$(P):GOSUB 150:T$=A$
300 Q$="Is the animal you are thinking of"+A$:GOSUB 100
310 IF A=1 THEN PRINT:PRINT"I got it!!!":GOTO 430
320 REM ** Learn a new animal
330 PRINT:PRINT"I give up!!!":PRINT "What is your animal ";:INPUT N$
340 A$=N$:GOSUB 150
350 PRINT:PRINT "Please enter a question that would distinguish" :PRIN
T "between"; A$;" and";T$:INPUT D$
360 Q$="For"+T$+" the answer would be":GOSUB 100
370 A$=T$(P):T$(P)=D$:T$(C+1)=A$:T$(C+2)=N$
380 IF A=1 THEN Y(P)=C+1:N(P)=C+2
390 IF A=0 THEN Y(P)=C+2:N(P)=C+1
400 Y(C+1)=0:N(C+1)=0:Y(C+2)=0:N(C+2)=0
410 C=C+2
420 REM ** End game & loop for another go
430 A=INT(C/2)+1
440 PRINT:PRINT"I now know ";A;" different Animals !"
450 GOTO 190
460 REM ** Initial Data
470 DATA 2,3,"Does it live in the water"
480 DATA 0,0,"Whale"
490 DATA 0,0,"Lion"
```

CODES AND SIGNALS

◄A string telephone is an easy signalling device to make and use.

We can send messages over long or short distances in a number of different ways. Most often, we use the telephone. This type of voice message travels as an electrical signal along metal wires between the two telephones, or as a radio signal in the case of radiotelephones.

Picture messages can be added to sound messages by the use of television. Even newer is the use of lasers for sending messages and signals. In a laser beam, a word message is carried as light waves.

To send a secret message, a code is necessary. Whoever is to receive the message needs to have the key of the code in order to understand the message. But it is possible to 'crack' secret codes, as shown below. The systems of signalling known as Morse and semaphore, use a special sign code to send all kinds of signals, secret or otherwise.

To make a string telephone you need two tin cans and some thin, tough string or twine. Make a hole in the bottom of each can, insert the string, knotting the end to stop the string pulling through. Then use the open end of the cans as ear- or mouth-pieces of a telephone to talk to a friend, with the string pulled taut

---

Morse Code

short flash ● long flash ▬

A	B	C	D	E	F	G
▬●	▬●●●	▬●▬●	▬●●	●	●●▬●	▬▬●
H	I	J	K	L	M	N
●●●●	●●	●▬▬▬	▬●▬	●▬●●	▬▬	▬●
O	P	Q	R	S	T	U
▬▬▬	●▬▬●	▬▬●▬	●▬●	●●●	▬	●●▬
V	W	X	Y	Z		
●●●▬	●▬▬	▬●●▬	▬●▬▬	▬▬●●		

1	2	3	4	5
●▬▬▬▬	●●▬▬▬	●●●▬▬	●●●●▬	●●●●●
6	7	8	9	10
▬●●●●	▬▬●●●	▬▬▬●●	▬▬▬▬●	▬▬▬▬▬

▲The Morse code is a way of sending messages using long and short flashes of light. You can use a pocket torch or flashlight (**top**) or a special signalling lamp (**opposite top**).

►Laser beams are a very modern way of sending messages over long distances. A laser-beam message could even be bounced off the Moon and back!

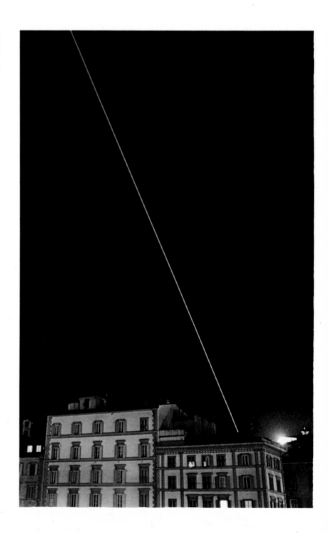

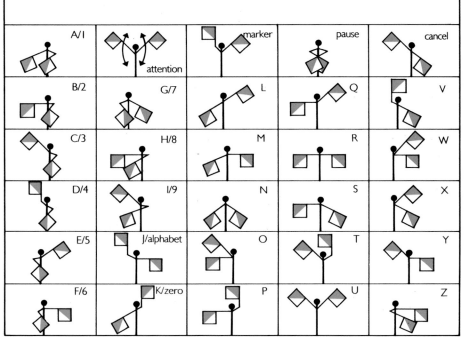

◄If you have no flashlight to hand, send a message in semaphore. Semaphore flags, as used traditionally by sailors, are a help, but you can semaphore using only your arms.

A keyword code – to send in morse or semaphore

Choose a keyword, for example LIBERTY. Write out the keyword followed by the whole of the alphabet. Cross out any repeated letters:

L I B E R T Y A B̶ C D E̶ F G H I̶ J K L̶ M N O P Q R̶ S T̶ U V W X Y̶ Z

Now write out the secret code, matching each letter against its alphabetic letter:

A	B	C	D	E	F	G	H	I	J	K	L	M	N	O	P	Q	R	S	T	U	V	W	X	Y	Z
L	I	B	E	R	T	Y	A	C	D	F	G	H	J	K	M	N	O	P	Q	S	U	V	W	X	Z

So, in this code, STATUE becomes PQLQSR

A grid reveals the secret

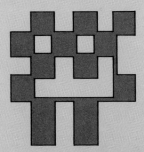

Decide on a cross-word-type grid with the friend who will receive the message. Cut out the grid in cardboard

T	R	H	M	E	F
P	M	O	E	S	E
T	N	I	T	N	G
G	P	L	A	C	Z
E	L	A	Q	S	U
S	F	U	T	A	L

The message you send will look a meaningless jumble of letters....

T		H	E		
	M	E		E	
T		I		N	G
	P	L	A	C	
E		A		S	U
S		U		A	L

....but all will be revealed when you put the grid over it!

Cracking a code

The best way is to work out the frequency with which certain letters occur in the coded message, then match these with the letters that occur most often in English. In order of frequency the nine most used letters in English are: E T A O N I S R H (Notice that these are the simplest to send in Morse because they need to be used most often.) When the letters are matched in this way the message often 'appears' in ordinary English, although some letters will have to be guessed, eg STAT**S**E O**T** A**I**C**E**RT**G** (Statue of Liberty)

COLLECTING MINERALS

▼Collecting minerals is good fun, excellent exercise and instructive! What's more, the most expensive item of equipment you will need is a stout pair of boots, everything else is quite cheap.

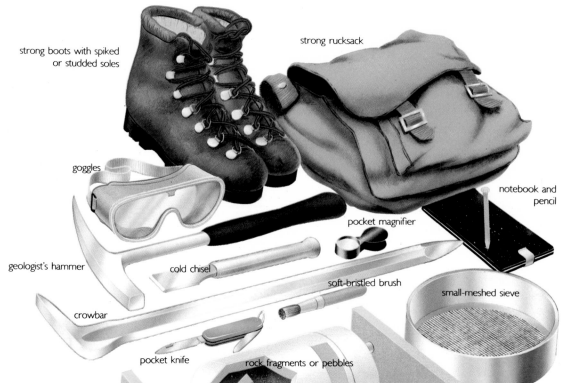

strong boots with spiked or studded soles

strong rucksack

goggles

notebook and pencil

pocket magnifier

geologist's hammer

cold chisel

soft-bristled brush

small-meshed sieve

crowbar

pocket knife

rock fragments or pebbles

metal ring bearing round metal shaft

wooden shaft with ribbed rubber hose glued over it

strong wooden frame

silicon carbide grit

large pulley

grade 80

pulley belt

grade 220

small pulley

electric motor

tumbler barrel

grade 400

tin oxide or cerium oxide polish

Tumble polish your minerals

▶1 Fill tumbler barrel ⅔ full with stones to be polished, cover them with water, add a tablespoon of silicon carbide abrasive, grade 80. Rotate barrel for a week, or until stones are smooth and rounded. Add more 80-grade silicon carbide if the stones are not becoming smooth.
2 Remove and wash stones, wash out barrel. Refill with stones and water. Add a tablespoon of grade 220 silicon carbide abrasive. Rotate for 120 hours, or 5 days and nights.
3 Wash stones and barrel. Refill. Add a tablespoon of grade 400 silicon carbide abrasive. Tumble again for 120 hours.
4 Wash stones and barrel well, then tumble with a small amount of a polishing agent, eg tin oxide or cerium oxide, for 2–3 days.
5 Tumble for a few hours in detergent and water.

Experts collect rocks, stones and pebbles as part of the science of *geology*, the study of the Earth. But you don't have to be a geologist to enjoy collecting minerals. Many are very attractive, but they can be made even nicer, smooth and shiny, by the art of lapidary, or cutting and polishing. Suitable rocks to polish are the not-so-hard ones such as agates and serpentine – as any lapidary book will tell you.

Moh's scale – testing minerals for hardness

Moh's scale number		typical mineral	simple hardness tests
Hardest	10	diamond →	scratches all other minerals
	9	sapphire	scratched by diamond but too precious
	8	topaz	for hardness testing!
	7	quartz →	scratched by a hard steel file
	6	feldspar →	scratched by quartz
	5	apatite →	scratched by penknife
	4	fluorite →	scratched by glass
	3	calcite →	scratched by copper coin
softest	2	gypsum →	scratched by finger nail
	1	talc →	crumbles between fingers

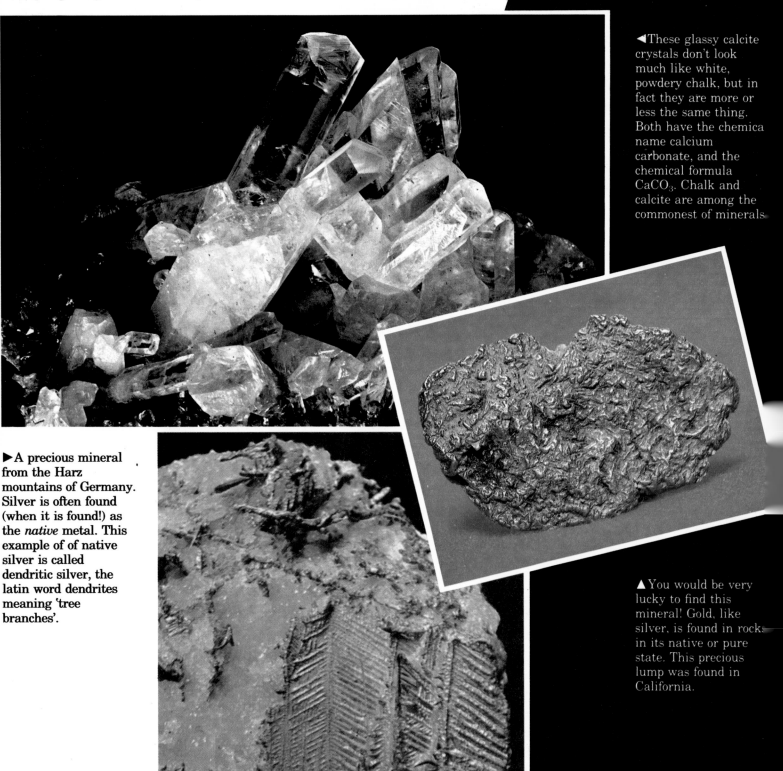

◀These glassy calcite crystals don't look much like white, powdery chalk, but in fact they are more or less the same thing. Both have the chemical name calcium carbonate, and the chemical formula $CaCO_3$. Chalk and calcite are among the commonest of minerals.

▶A precious mineral from the Harz mountains of Germany. Silver is often found (when it is found!) as the *native* metal. This example of of native silver is called dendritic silver, the latin word dendrites meaning 'tree branches'.

▲You would be very lucky to find this mineral! Gold, like silver, is found in rocks in its native or pure state. This precious lump was found in California.

▲This limestone rock is crowded with fossil shellfish of the kind known as gastropods. These are very similar to the whelks and sea-snails still living today. In fact, the rock is quite young by geological standards – not more than 60 million years old.

▼This fossil plant comes from the *Tertiary* period, the same geological period as the gastropods (**top**). This was the age when such modern creatures as mammals, and such modern plants as flowers, first appeared.

▶Brittlestars are long-armed relatives of starfish. These fossil brittlestars are far more ancient than the other two types of fossil. They come from the *Devonian* period, which began 400 million years ago.

Fossil-collecting, like rock-collecting, must have been popular with people for as long as history. But *fossils* were regarded as mysterious objects until about two centuries ago. Then scientists explained them as the remains of animals and plants that long ago had lived on Earth but has died out or become extinct, leaving behind them only their traces in the rocks.

Usually, only the skeleton and other hard parts of an animal are found as fossils, though plants with a woody 'skeleton' sometimes leave an almost complete fossil.

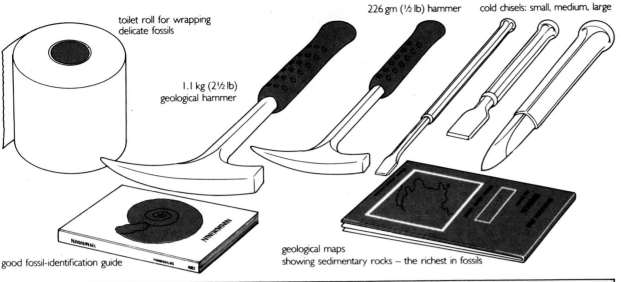

toilet roll for wrapping
delicate fossils

1.1 kg (2½ lb)
geological hammer

226 gm (½ lb) hammer

cold chisels: small, medium, large

good fossil-identification guide

geological maps
showing sedimentary rocks – the richest in fossils

◀Fossil-collecting equipment is similar to rock-collecting, but you will need a good geological map. If you live in the USA, buy one from The US Geological Survey, Washington 25, DC. In the UK, get your map from The Institute of Geological Sciences, Exhibition Road, South Kensington, London SW7 2DE.

a Good places for finding fossils

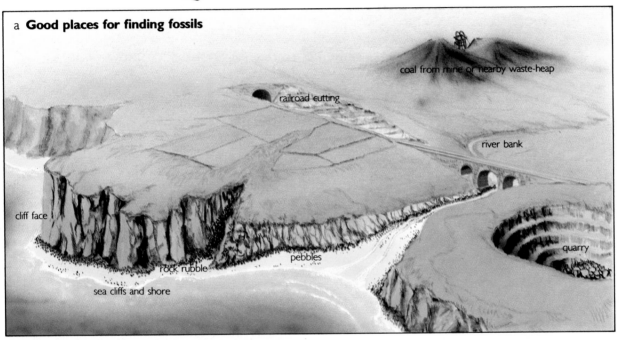

coal from mine or nearby waste-heap

railroad cutting

river bank

cliff face

quarry

rock rubble

pebbles

sea cliffs and shore

◀Excellent places to find fossils include the faces of sea cliffs and quarries. You will find other fossils by cracking seashore pebbles and fallen rocks. Coal mines are very rich in fossils because coal itself is a fossil fuel'– sometimes whole tree trunks are preserved in the coal seams. If you don't live near any such places, try searching river banks and railroad cuttings for fossils, always remembering that you may have to crack a stone to find one, and taking care not to trespass.

b Removing fossils from hard rock

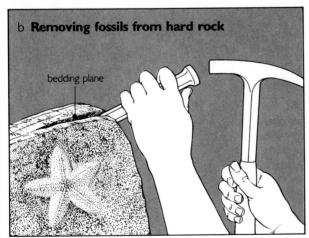

bedding plane

c Removing fossils from ironstone

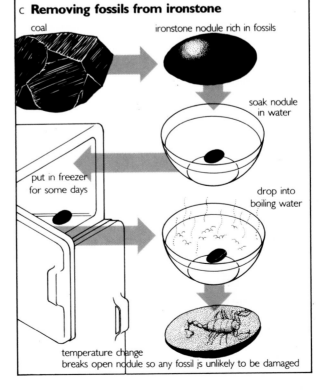

coal

ironstone nodule rich in fossils

soak nodule in water

put in freezer for some days

drop into boiling water

temperature change breaks open nodule so any fossil is unlikely to be damaged

d **Removing a small fossil from soft rock**

▲To free a large fossil from hard rock, chisel into the *bedding plane* (direction in which the rock splits most easily) until the fossil comes away undamaged.

▶Ironstone nodules in coal seams often contain fossil insects. Use this special technique to crack open the nodule at the right place.

▲To free a small fossil in a soft rock such as chalk, gouge away with a penknife at a safe distance all around the fossil, until it comes free.

RECOGNIZE STARS AND PLANETS

A simple telescope, or a pair of field glasses or binoculars, will show you far more stars than you can see with the naked eye. Focus your telescope on the Moon and you will be able to see details of its craters, seas or *mares*, and other features (remember, the Moon always shows you the same face).

You can identify planets by their size and brilliance, and by the way they apparently wander in an irregular motion among the 'fixed' stars.

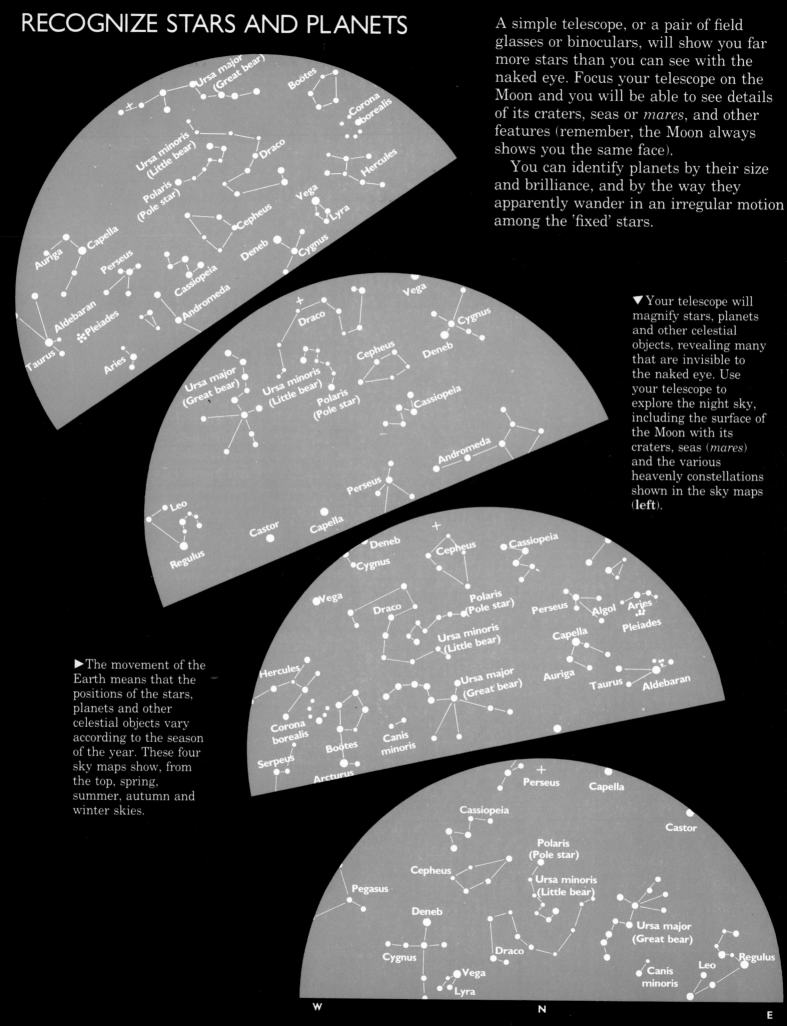

▼Your telescope will magnify stars, planets and other celestial objects, revealing many that are invisible to the naked eye. Use your telescope to explore the night sky, including the surface of the Moon with its craters, seas (*mares*) and the various heavenly constellations shown in the sky maps (**left**).

▶The movement of the Earth means that the positions of the stars, planets and other celestial objects vary according to the season of the year. These four sky maps show, from the top, spring, summer, autumn and winter skies.

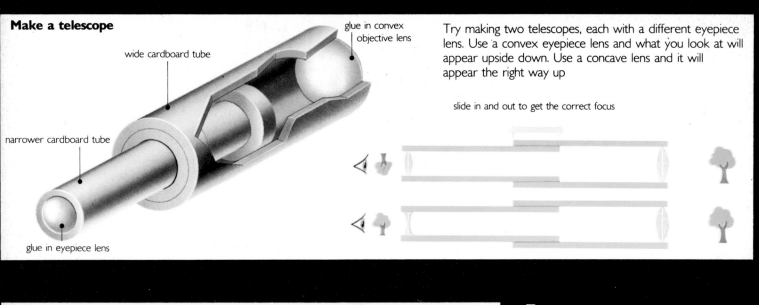

Make a telescope

wide cardboard tube

glue in convex objective lens

narrower cardboard tube

glue in eyepiece lens

Try making two telescopes, each with a different eyepiece lens. Use a convex eyepiece lens and what you look at will appear upside down. Use a concave lens and it will appear the right way up

slide in and out to get the correct focus

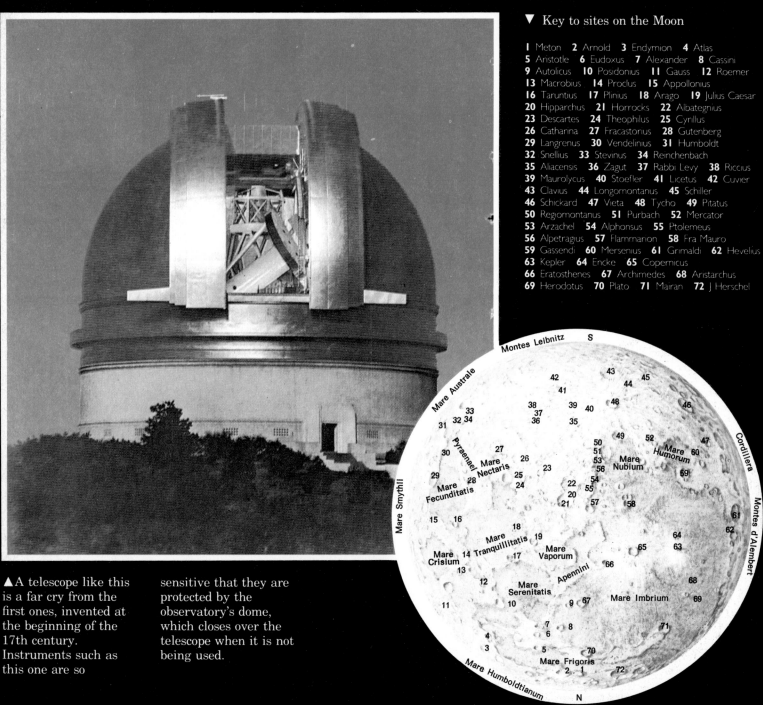

▼ Key to sites on the Moon

1 Meton 2 Arnold 3 Endymion 4 Atlas
5 Aristotle 6 Eudoxus 7 Alexander 8 Cassini
9 Autolicus 10 Posidonius 11 Gauss 12 Roemer
13 Macrobius 14 Proclus 15 Appollonius
16 Taruntius 17 Plinius 18 Arago 19 Julius Caesar
20 Hipparchus 21 Horrocks 22 Albategnius
23 Descartes 24 Theophilus 25 Cyrillus
26 Catharina 27 Fracastorius 28 Gutenberg
29 Langrenus 30 Vendelinius 31 Humboldt
32 Snellius 33 Stevinus 34 Reinchenbach
35 Aliacensis 36 Zagut 37 Rabbi Levy 38 Riccius
39 Maurolycus 40 Stoefler 41 Licetus 42 Cuvier
43 Clavius 44 Longomontanus 45 Schiller
46 Schickard 47 Vieta 48 Tycho 49 Pitatus
50 Regiomontanus 51 Purbach 52 Mercator
53 Arzachel 54 Alphonsus 55 Ptolemeus
56 Alpetragius 57 Flammarion 58 Fra Mauro
59 Gassendi 60 Mersenius 61 Grimaldi 62 Hevelius
63 Kepler 64 Encke 65 Copernicus
66 Eratosthenes 67 Archimedes 68 Aristarchus
69 Herodotus 70 Plato 71 Mairan 72 J Herschel

▲A telescope like this is a far cry from the first ones, invented at the beginning of the 17th century. Instruments such as this one are so sensitive that they are protected by the observatory's dome, which closes over the telescope when it is not being used.

3 EXPERIMENTS AND INVENTIONS

to embalm their dead, to make glass, and to prepare cosmetics. A thousand years ago, the first firework celebrations were held by the Chinese, who had invented gunpowder – but later civilizations used it for warfare.

Modern chemistry provides us with many of our modern needs, from nylon shirts and plastic goods to automobile fuels and detergents. In nearly every branch of industry, products are chemically tested before being sent out from the factory.

SOME CHEMICAL TESTS

Chemistry helped make civilizations. More than four thousand years ago, the ancient Egyptians used their chemical knowledge

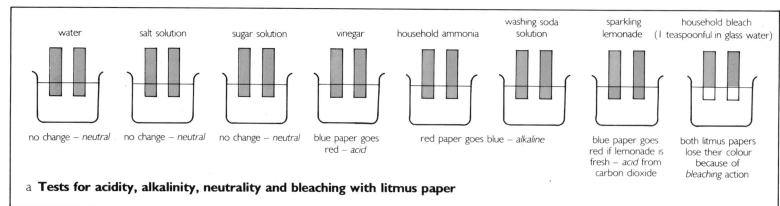

| water | salt solution | sugar solution | vinegar | household ammonia | washing soda solution | sparkling lemonade | household bleach (1 teaspoonful in glass water) |

no change – *neutral* · no change – *neutral* · no change – *neutral* · blue paper goes red – *acid* · red paper goes blue – *alkaline* · blue paper goes red if lemonade is fresh – *acid* from carbon dioxide · both litmus papers lose their colour because of *bleaching* action

a **Tests for acidity, alkalinity, neutrality and bleaching with litmus paper**

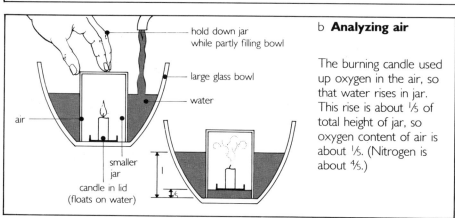

b **Analyzing air**

- hold down jar while partly filling bowl
- large glass bowl
- water
- air
- smaller jar
- candle in lid (floats on water)

The burning candle used up oxygen in the air, so that water rises in jar. This rise is about 1/5 of total height of jar, so oxygen content of air is about 1/5. (Nitrogen is about 4/5.)

c **Analyzing water by electrolysis**

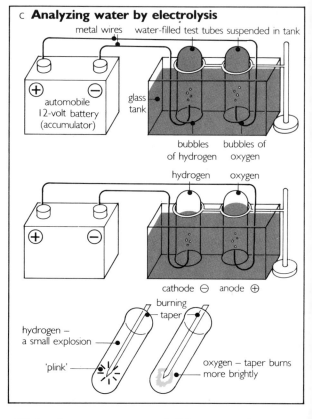

- metal wires
- water-filled test tubes suspended in tank
- automobile 12-volt battery (accumulator)
- glass tank
- bubbles of hydrogen
- bubbles of oxygen
- hydrogen
- oxygen
- cathode ⊖
- anode ⊕
- burning taper
- hydrogen – a small explosion
- 'plink'
- oxygen – taper burns more brightly

◄Nature's own chemistry – a salt workings at Lanzarote, Canary Islands.

►More natural chemistry – *stalactites* and *stalagmites* formed from calcium carbonate.

SOME PHYSICAL TESTS

We take most of the things around us for granted, but if asked to explain them, are often stumped for an answer. More often than not, the problem we are facing is one in physics. Why do small insects get trapped in the surface water of ponds? Why can we move a heavy rock with the aid of a lever, when it defeats our strength otherwise? How does an airplane, heavier than air, stay up? Not all these questions are equally easy to answer – physics can be quite difficult to study. Often, though, it is surprisingly easy to demonstrate some principle of physics by quite a simple test, which can be both useful and amusing.

a Testing for inertia

When the paper is pulled slowly the book moves with it. But when the paper is snatched away the book is left behind on the table by its own inertia or resistance to movement. This is also the basis for the waiter's famous trick

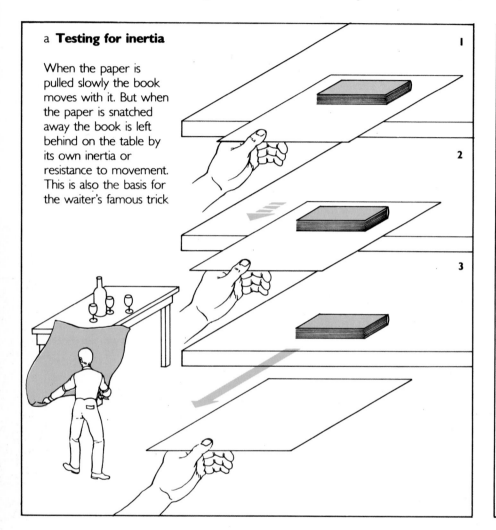

b Testing for surface tension

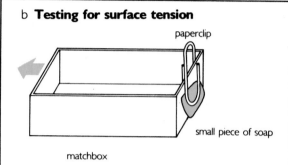

paperclip

matchbox

small piece of soap

You may have seen a fly or some other small insect struggling to free itself from the surface of water. The force that keeps it 'sticking' to the water is called surface tension. It is the result of the forces of attraction between water *molecules*. To demonstrate this force, attach a small piece of soap to a matchbox or a square of polystyrene cut from a polystyrene cup, with a paperclip as shown. Fill a bowl or basin with hot water and wait until the water's surface is still. Float the matchbox on the surface. It will soon start to move because soap dissolving in the warm water reduces the surface tension in the area under the matchbox. Therefore the forces on the water's surface are unequal, and so the resulting force pulls the matchbox along. In a minute or two the matchbox will stop moving because the surface tension over the whole surface of the water has been reduced and is once again equal all over, so there is no force to pull the matchbox along.

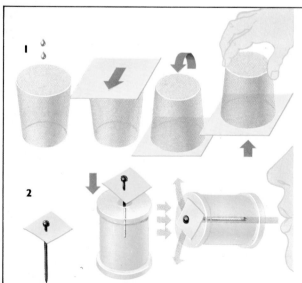

c Two tests for air pressure

Air presses all around us, so that each square centimetre (or square inch) of our body receives pressure of about 1.05 kg (15 lb)! But this air pressure acts both inside and outside our body, so that is why we do not feel it.

1 Fill a tumbler brimful with water. Slide a piece of glossy (shiny) paper over the glass. Very carefully turn the glass upside down and rest in on a table or other firm flat surface. Lift the glass – air pressure should hold paper and water in place. (But have a cloth handy, just in case!)

2 Stick a pin through a small piece of paper, then insert pin and paper into the central hole of an empty cotton reel and blow down the other end of the hole. You won't be able to blow the paper away. Why? The reason is that as you blow air rushes out between the paper and the cotton reel, so reducing the air pressure there. For this reason, the harder you blow, the firmer the paper is held in place by normal air pressure on the other side of the paper.

▼Surface tension in water is a physical force caused by the attraction of water molecules for each other. Drops of water are rounded up by this force on the waxy surface of a water plant's leaf (**inset**). Surface tension can trap many small insects, but the midge laying its eggs in the water (**below**), has nothing to fear. It dips only the tips of its long legs into the water's surface, and these, like the waxy plant leaf, repel water.

◄To measure the hardness of a sample of metal, a diamond-tipped steel column is pushed into the sample with a known force. The deeper the column goes, the softer the metal. Diamond is harder than any metal, as shown by the Moh's Scale – see page 19.

◄Archimedes, seated at the table, is the most famous of early Greek physicists and mathematicians. In physics he discovered the principle of *specific gravity* (*relative density*) while taking his bath. According to tradition, he jumped out, shouting 'Eureka!' or 'I've found it!' He also said, talking of levers, 'Give me a place to stand on, and I will move the world'. This mosaic picture shows his last moments. The Romans had invaded Syracuse, Sicily, where Archimedes lived. Some of his inventions had been used against the Romans by the city's defenders. When Archimedes refused to leave his work, the Romans killed him.

TESTING MAGNETISM

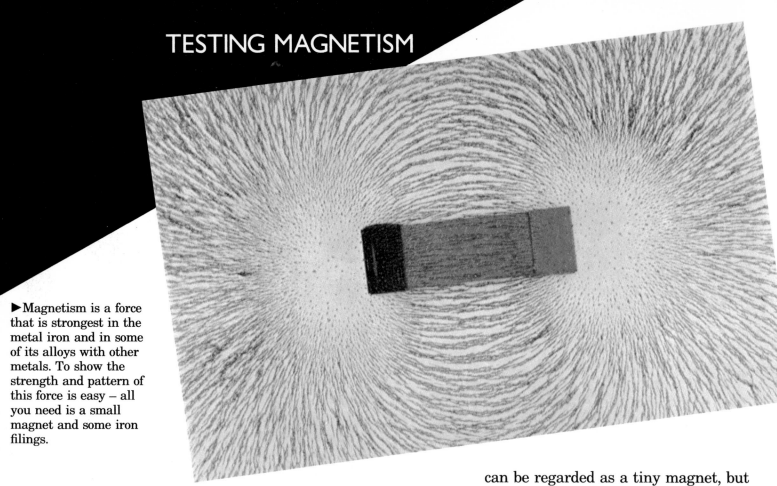

▶Magnetism is a force that is strongest in the metal iron and in some of its alloys with other metals. To show the strength and pattern of this force is easy – all you need is a small magnet and some iron filings.

Most people know what a magnet is, yet how many people can explain magnetism or magnetic force? A full explanation is quite a difficult matter even for a scientist. It requires, first of all, a knowledge of *atoms* and the *electrons* that spin inside them. Each spinning electron can be regarded as a tiny magnet, but inside an atom electrons spin in different directions and so their magnetism is cancelled out. In some metals, however, the spins of many electrons all line up in the same direction, so that their magnetic force adds up to make the metal strongly magnetic. Iron and its *alloys* are the most strongly magnetic materials.

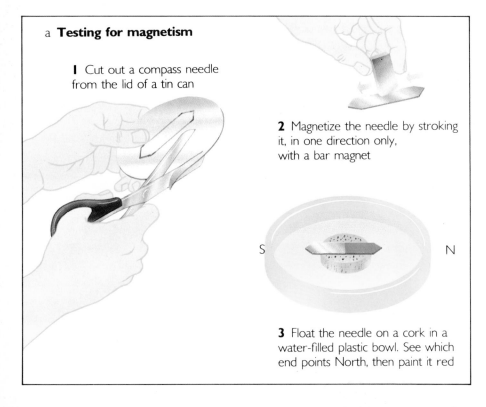

a Testing for magnetism

1 Cut out a compass needle from the lid of a tin can

2 Magnetize the needle by stroking it, in one direction only, with a bar magnet

S   N

3 Float the needle on a cork in a water-filled plastic bowl. See which end points North, then paint it red

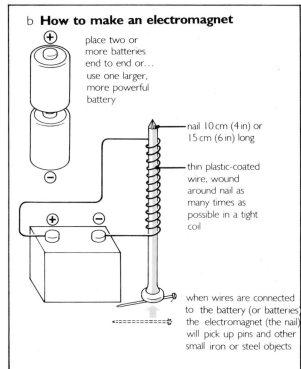

b How to make an electromagnet

(+)

place two or more batteries end to end or... use one larger, more powerful battery

(−)

nail 10 cm (4 in) or 15 cm (6 in) long

thin plastic-coated wire, wound around nail as many times as possible in a tight coil

(+)   (−)

when wires are connected to the battery (or batteries) the electromagnet (the nail) will pick up pins and other small iron or steel objects

◄Magnetism was well-known to the ancients. Over a thousand years ago the Chinese invented the magnetic compass. Its metal needle always points north-south, in the direction of the Earth's own magnetic field. This traveller's compass dates from 1660 and was made by the Englishman Henry Sutton. Its case also contains a sundial for telling the hours.

▼How do migrating birds, such as these geese, find their way? Very probably they can sense the direction of the Earth's magnetic field, which helps them to navigate perhaps thousands of miles in the right direction.

TESTING ELECTRICITY

▼The metal ball the girl is touching is highly charged with electricity. This causes her hair to become charged too, and since like charges repel one another (see **opposite top**) her hair stands on end. Caution – never touch a high voltage electrical wire to get similar results!

Our houses are lighted, and perhaps heated too, by electricity. In our homes we use electrical gadgets ranging from food mixers to radios and TV. The electricity for these and other purposes is made in power stations, from which tall pylons and their high-voltage metal cables carry electrical current to town and factory.

Electrical current is a flow of electrons or negatively-charged particles. Electricity can also exist as static electricity or electrical charge, in which the electrons are stationary, as on the metal ball and rubber balloons in the pictures.

▼Lightning flashes are caused by the build-up of electrical charges in thunder clouds. When the build-up has reached a very high level, the electrical resistance of the air is overcome and a flash of a million or more *volts* results.

a Testing for static electricity

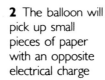

2 The balloon will pick up small pieces of paper with an opposite electrical charge

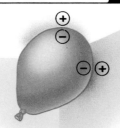

3 For the same reason, the balloon will be attracted to and stick to wallpaper and the ceiling

1 Rub an inflated balloon against your (*dry*) sweater. This causes the surface of the balloon to become electrically charged

4 Opposite electrical charges attract, but like electrical charges repel. So two balloons charged in the same way will move away from each other

b Testing electrical flow and resistance

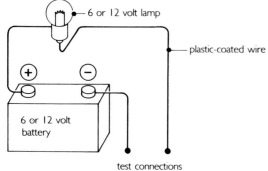

— 6 or 12 volt lamp

— plastic-coated wire

(+)   (−)

6 or 12 volt battery

test connections

Make the electrical tester as shown above and then connect the materials shown on the right to the tester. If the lamp lights, then electric current is flowing through it and so the material is an electric conductor. If the lamp fails to light, then little or no electricity is flowing, because the material has high *electrical resistance*.

1 plastic strip

2 metal strip

3 porcelain

4 distilled water

5 salt water

6 paraffin fuel
*take care no flame is near

►Among the many kinds of machine powered by electricity is this large industrial blower or fan. The technician beside it gives an idea of its size.

MAKING AN ALLOY

►An ancient Chinese bronze jar. The Chinese were the first to use bronze alloy for such large and heavy objects. Archaeologists know that some of these vessels are at least 3,000 years old.

▼A Roman blacksmith would have used tools such as these about 2,000 years ago. They were of wrought iron – the alloy mild steel had not yet been invented.

Alloys are made by mixing metals, sometimes with other metals, sometimes with non-metals, sometimes with both. One example of a metal-metal alloy is brass, which is a mixture of copper and zinc, but is tougher and harder-wearing than either of its 'parent' metals.

This extra strength is one reason for making alloys. Brass was used in past centuries to make scientific instruments such as telescopes and the cases for magnetic compasses, which had to stay reliable when exposed to the weather for many years. This is another reason for making alloys – they are often much less liable to corrode, or 'rust' as we say of iron alloys, when exposed to wind, rain and corrosive gases such as those given off from factory chimneys.

The most widely-used alloy of all is steel, which is made by mixing iron with small amounts of non-metals, mainly carbon. Mild steel is made in this way. Even stronger, more corrosion-resistant, special steels also contain other metals, such as nickel, chromium and molybdenum. Mild steel is used to make most kinds of large, heavy metal structures such as bridges and industrial tanks or containers. For more lightweight structures, the most frequently used alloys are those of aluminum. For example, if you own a stereo or radio, it will probably be made largely from lightweight aluminum-magnesium alloy.

Most alloys cannot be made at home because their melting temperatures are too high – you would need a special furnace to make them. However, alloys of lead, tin, bismuth, cadmium and a few other metals melt at much lower temperatures, easily obtained with a simple bunsen burner.

◄These four Bronze Age weapons were made about 4,000 years ago. Notice how much simpler they are than the Chinese vessel (**top**).

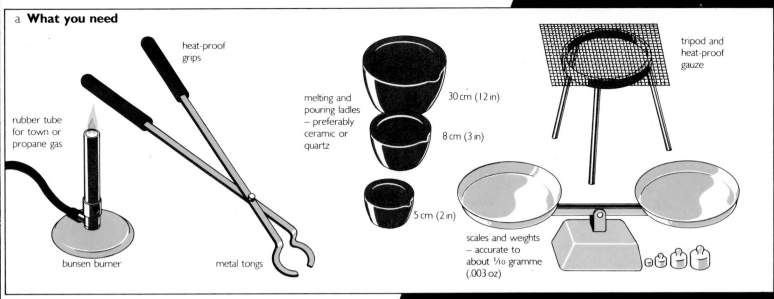

heat-proof grips

rubber tube for town or propane gas

melting and pouring ladles – preferably ceramic or quartz

30 cm (12 in)

8 cm (3 in)

5 cm (2 in)

tripod and heat-proof gauze

bunsen burner

metal tongs

scales and weights – accurate to about ¹/₁₀ gramme (.003 oz)

b **Metals and where to get them**

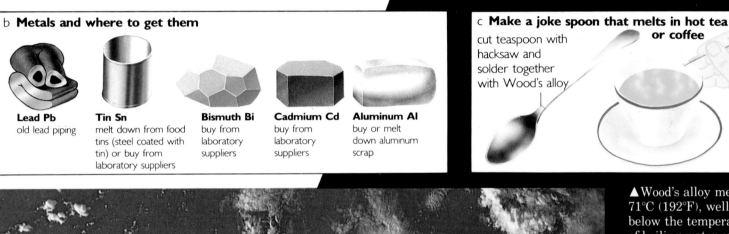

Lead Pb
old lead piping

Tin Sn
melt down from food tins (steel coated with tin) or buy from laboratory suppliers

Bismuth Bi
buy from laboratory suppliers

Cadmium Cd
buy from laboratory suppliers

Aluminum Al
buy or melt down aluminum scrap

c **Make a joke spoon that melts in hot tea or coffee**

cut teaspoon with hacksaw and solder together with Wood's alloy

▲Wood's alloy melts at 71°C (192°F), well below the temperature of boiling water or hot tea. You can make it by melting together 4 parts by weight of bismuth, 2 parts of lead, 1 part of tin and 1 part of cadmium. If you can't get cadmium, you could make Rose's alloy, which melts at 94°C (233°F). This requires 2 parts of bismuth, 1 part of lead, and 1 part of tin.

◄Space vehicles need many special alloys, some to withstand very high temperatures without melting, and others, inside the craft, to ensure that the complicated instruments work absolutely correctly.

We need light for vision. The eyes of totally blind people cannot receive light, so they cannot see either the world's beauties or its dangers.

Light travels to our eyes not only from here on Earth, but from everywhere in the universe. It even reaches us from the farthest stars.

Humans have *binocular vision* – we use both of our eyes at once to see in depth. This is not so for many other animals, such as the horses on the opposite page. We also have colour vision – but the owl does not.

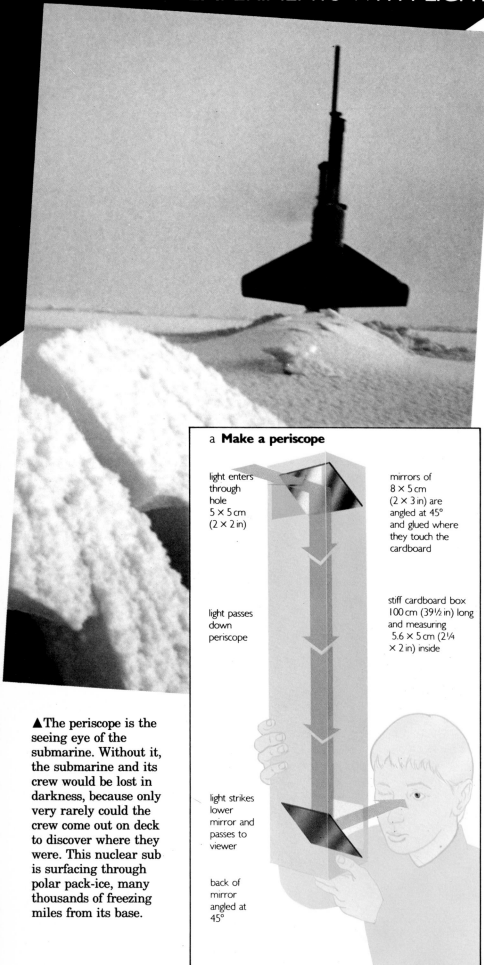

▲The periscope is the seeing eye of the submarine. Without it, the submarine and its crew would be lost in darkness, because only very rarely could the crew come out on deck to discover where they were. This nuclear sub is surfacing through polar pack-ice, many thousands of freezing miles from its base.

a **Make a periscope**

light enters through hole 5 × 5 cm (2 × 2 in)

mirrors of 8 × 5 cm (2 × 3 in) are angled at 45° and glued where they touch the cardboard

light passes down periscope

stiff cardboard box 100 cm (39½ in) long and measuring 5.6 × 5 cm (2¼ × 2 in) inside

light strikes lower mirror and passes to viewer

back of mirror angled at 45°

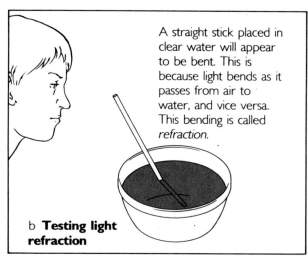

A straight stick placed in clear water will appear to be bent. This is because light bends as it passes from air to water, and vice versa. This bending is called *refraction*.

b **Testing light refraction**

c **The phantom floating sausage**

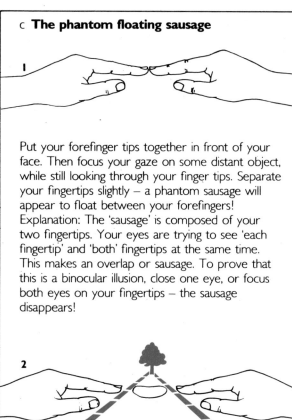

Put your forefinger tips together in front of your face. Then focus your gaze on some distant object, while still looking through your finger tips. Separate your fingertips slightly – a phantom sausage will appear to float between your forefingers! Explanation: The 'sausage' is composed of your two fingertips. Your eyes are trying to see 'each fingertip' and 'both' fingertips at the same time. This makes an overlap or sausage. To prove that this is a binocular illusion, close one eye, or focus both eyes on your fingertips – the sausage disappears!

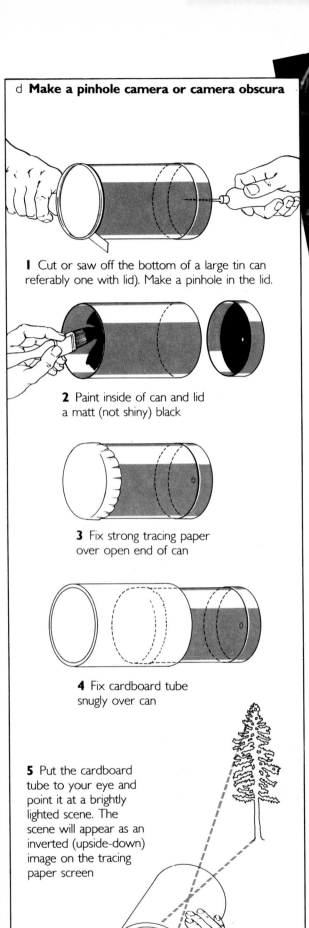

d Make a pinhole camera or camera obscura

1 Cut or saw off the bottom of a large tin can referably one with lid). Make a pinhole in the lid.

2 Paint inside of can and lid a matt (not shiny) black

3 Fix strong tracing paper over open end of can

4 Fix cardboard tube snugly over can

5 Put the cardboard tube to your eye and point it at a brightly lighted scene. The scene will appear as an inverted (upside-down) image on the tracing paper screen

◄A bittern takes a good look, using both eyes. Its binocular vision tells it just how far away any intruder might be.

▼The barn owl, like other owls, flies by night to catch its prey. It can see well enough to do this even in very poor light. On the other hand, the owl cannot see colour, but this is no drawback, because at night objects only appear black and white.

▼A horse does not have full binocular vision. Only part of what the horse sees is shared by both eyes. Blinkers, however, allow a horse to see only forwards.

EXPERIMENTS WITH COLOUR

We see colours because the retinas, sheets of tissue at the back of our eyes, have special light-sensitive cells that are particularly good at detecting light of particular wavelengths. Colour is simply the way in which the brain sees, or understands, these particular wavelengths. It is perhaps surprising that a mixture of coloured lights can go to make up white light. Well, make the Newton's disk below to prove it! More usually, as in painting, we mix different paints or pigments, and these will *never* add up to make 'white'.

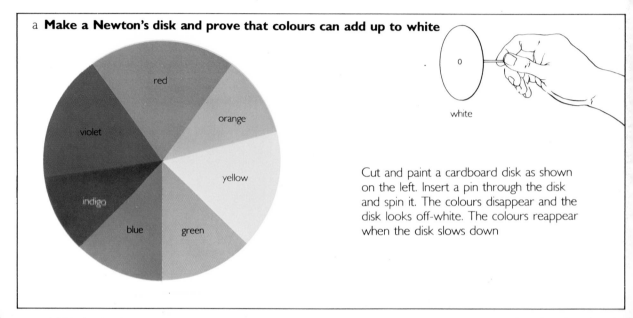

a Make a Newton's disk and prove that colours can add up to white

red
orange
violet
yellow
indigo
blue
green

white

Cut and paint a cardboard disk as shown on the left. Insert a pin through the disk and spin it. The colours disappear and the disk looks off-white. The colours reappear when the disk slows down

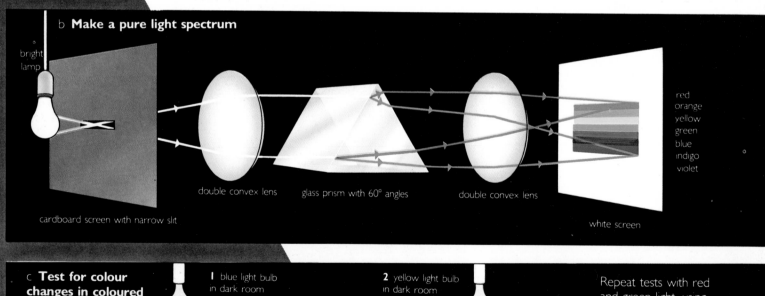

b Make a pure light spectrum

bright lamp

cardboard screen with narrow slit

double convex lens

glass prism with 60° angles

double convex lens

red
orange
yellow
green
blue
indigo
violet

white screen

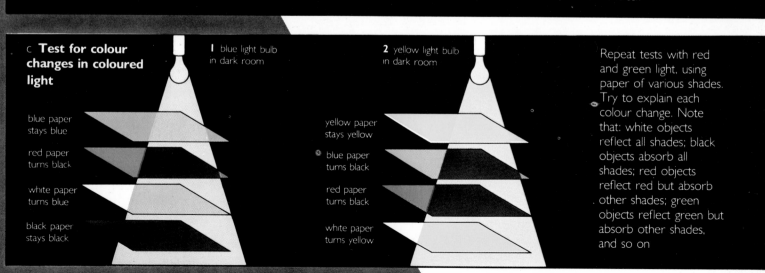

c Test for colour changes in coloured light

1 blue light bulb in dark room

2 yellow light bulb in dark room

blue paper stays blue

red paper turns black

white paper turns blue

black paper stays black

yellow paper stays yellow

blue paper turns black

red paper turns black

white paper turns yellow

Repeat tests with red and green light, using paper of various shades. Try to explain each colour change. Note that: white objects reflect all shades; black objects absorb all shades; red objects reflect red but absorb other shades; green objects reflect green but absorb other shades, and so on

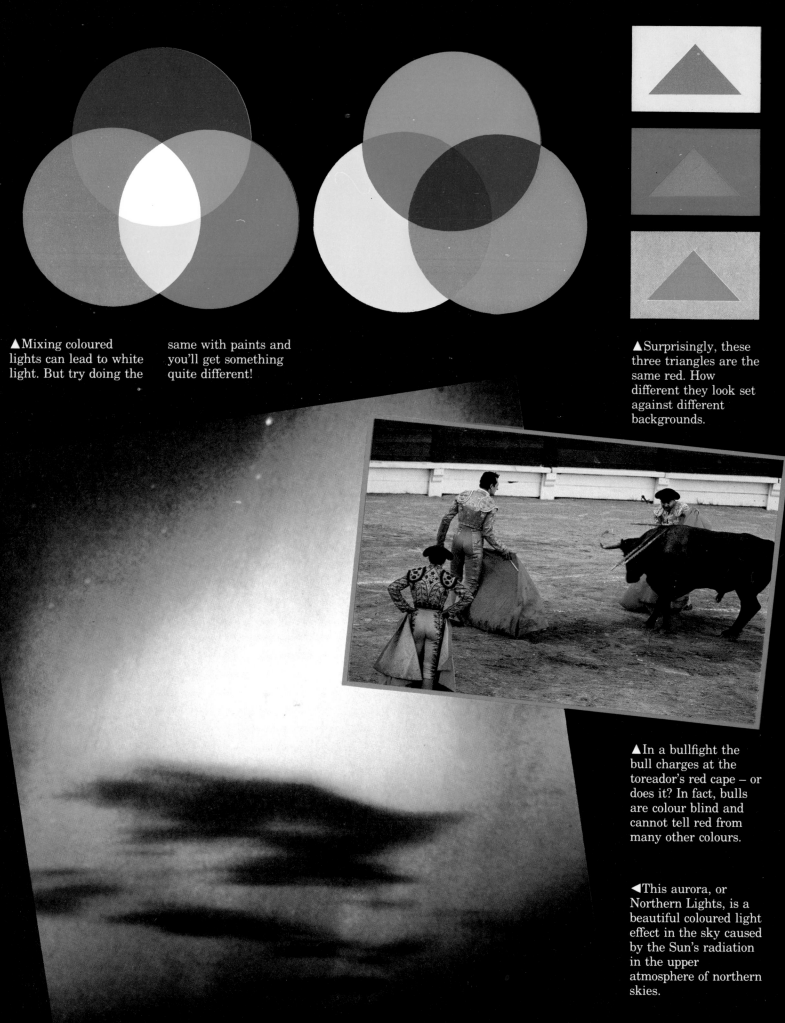

▲Mixing coloured lights can lead to white light. But try doing the same with paints and you'll get something quite different!

▲Surprisingly, these three triangles are the same red. How different they look set against different backgrounds.

▲In a bullfight the bull charges at the toreador's red cape – or does it? In fact, bulls are colour blind and cannot tell red from many other colours.

◄This aurora, or Northern Lights, is a beautiful coloured light effect in the sky caused by the Sun's radiation in the upper atmosphere of northern skies.

OPTICAL ILLUSIONS

a **Optical illusions**

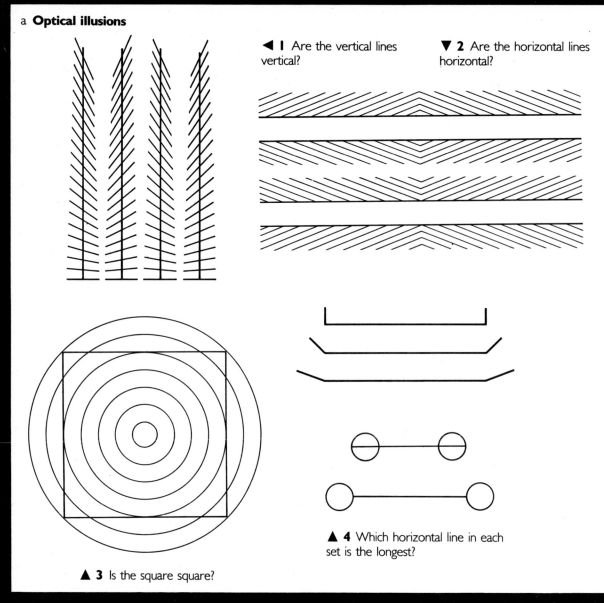

◄ **1** Are the vertical lines vertical?

▼ **2** Are the horizontal lines horizontal?

▲ **4** Which horizontal line in each set is the longest?

▲ **3** Is the square square?

b **An illusion with mirrors**

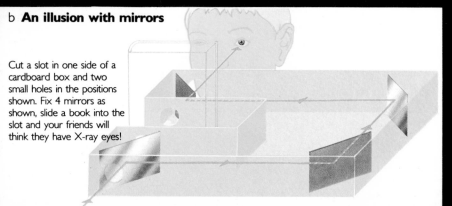

Cut a slot in one side of a cardboard box and two small holes in the positions shown. Fix 4 mirrors as shown, slide a book into the slot and your friends will think they have X-ray eyes!

c **An impossible shape that you can draw**

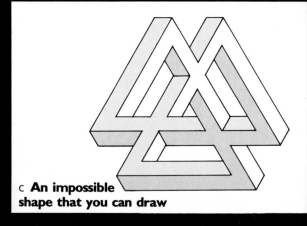

'Now you see it, now you don't.' Sometimes your brain can't quite make sense of what your eyes are seeing. This can either be a vision or hallucination, such as a ghost, which being 'unreal', is not easily explained by science. Or it can be an optical illusion, which *can* be explained scientifically. One example of an optical illusion that commonly deceives your eyes is the mirage. It's quite easy to create your own optical illusions. All you need to trick your own eyes and brain is pencil, paper, ruler, perhaps drawing compasses – and a steady hand!

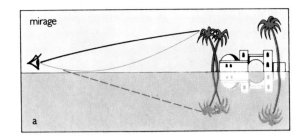

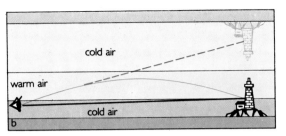

◀A mirage is caused by light bending when it passes from cool air to warm air and vice versa. Mirages are common over hot, flat areas such as deserts. In **a** the eye sees palm trees reflected in a 'pool'. In **b** it sees a floating upside-down lighthouse. **Below** is 'a lake that never was' – in reality a reflection of the sky.

▶A belvedere is a castle turret or a summerhouse from which you can enjoy the view. And that is exactly what the artist M.C. Escher has drawn here. Or is it? Look at the lower columns and the frame the man on the bench holds in his hands. The perspective is correct, the drawing superbly detailed, but oh, what an architect's nightmare – not to mention an optical illusion!

Answers to page 38

1 Yes
2 Yes
3 Yes
4 They are all the same length

TEST YOUR SENSES

Our five senses – sight, hearing, taste, smell and touch – tell us about the world around us. We talk of our senses as if they were quite separate from one another. But that is not so at all. Touch, for example, also includes the senses of heat and cold, tickle and pain. Taste is so strongly linked with smell that if your nose is blocked with a bad cold, you can 'taste' hardly anything, because both taste and smell go to make up flavours. Animals, such as the fly and fish opposite, have different senses and sense organs to our own.

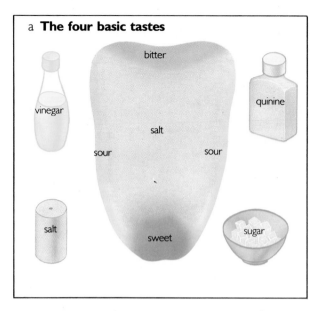

a **The four basic tastes**

b **What is hot and what is cold?**

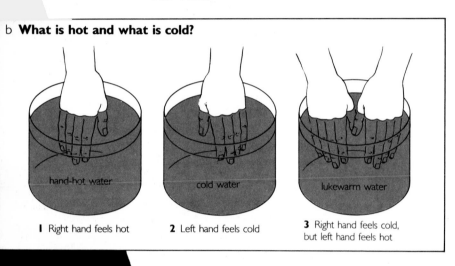

1 Right hand feels hot   **2** Left hand feels cold   **3** Right hand feels cold, but left hand feels hot

c **Seeing in depth**

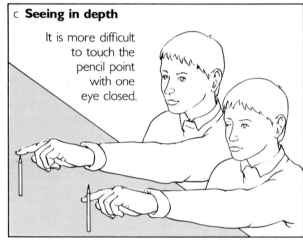

It is more difficult to touch the pencil point with one eye closed.

d **An ESP test – or can you read minds?**

Test your *extra-sensory perception* or ESP. Make a pack of ESP cards as shown. Shuffle the cards, pick one and concentrate hard on it for half a minute. A friend in the next room will try 'to receive' the picture of the card and sketch it in a notepad. Shuffle the cards again and pick another and concentrate on that. Repeat the experiment as many times as possible. Since there are 5 designs, the friend has a 1 in 5 chance of simply guessing the answer in each case. Thus, in 100 experiments, 20 correct answers would be the average due to chance. But to give the test any scientific value you would have to do it many, many times.

e **Test your touch sensitivity**

Where on your body can you feel the separate pencil points? These are the parts with the most nerve endings. Parts where you cannot tell that there are *two* pencil points have few nerve endings.

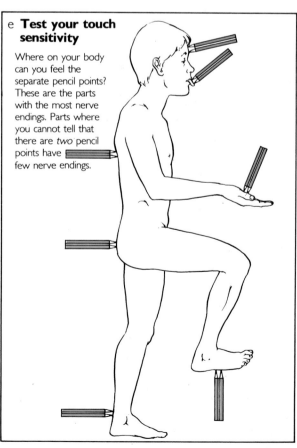

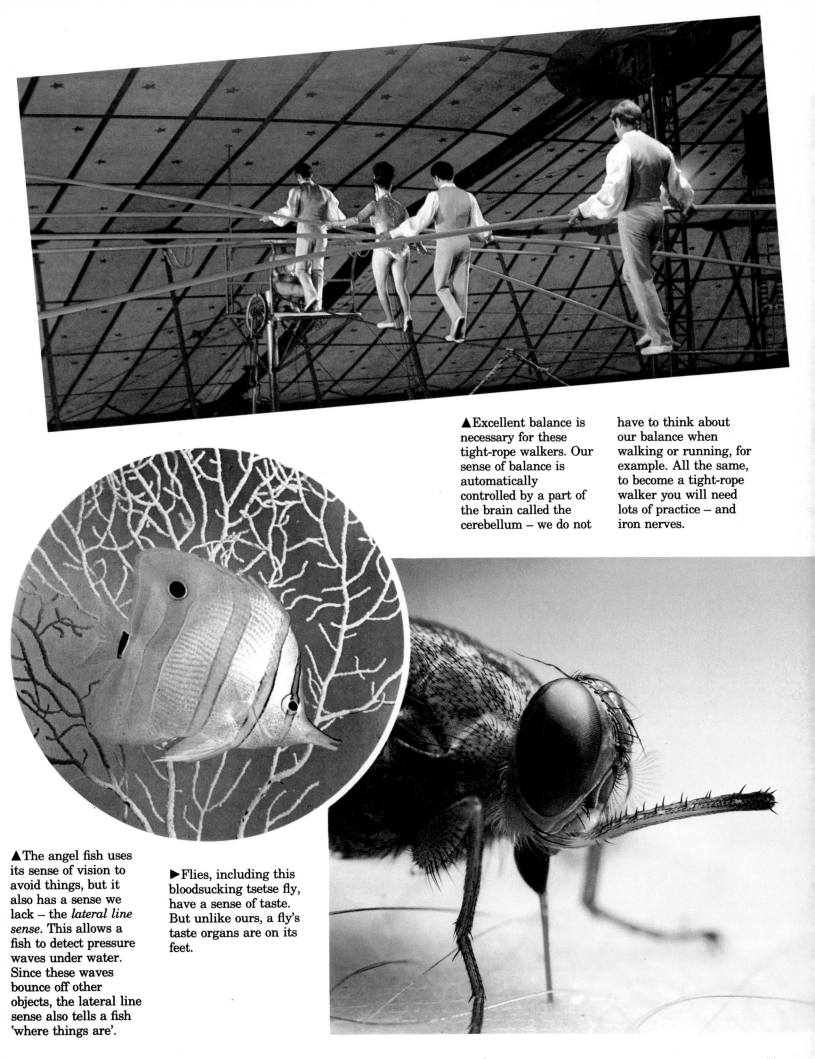

▲Excellent balance is necessary for these tight-rope walkers. Our sense of balance is automatically controlled by a part of the brain called the cerebellum – we do not have to think about our balance when walking or running, for example. All the same, to become a tight-rope walker you will need lots of practice – and iron nerves.

▲The angel fish uses its sense of vision to avoid things, but it also has a sense we lack – the *lateral line sense*. This allows a fish to detect pressure waves under water. Since these waves bounce off other objects, the lateral line sense also tells a fish 'where things are'.

▶Flies, including this bloodsucking tsetse fly, have a sense of taste. But unlike ours, a fly's taste organs are on its feet.

DETECTIVE WORK

◄Sherlock Holmes is the most famous detective in fiction, and many of the stories have been made into movies. Often Holmes solved complicated crimes on his own, often by fantastic guesswork. (Dr Watson, his friend and admirer, rarely had any very good ideas.) When in need of inspiration, Sherlock Holmes played the violin. Real detectives, however, usually work in a team – and a real-life Dr Watson would be a forensic scientist.

▼A dog's sense of smell is far more sensitive than our own, which makes dogs very useful in detective work. In Sherlock Holmes' day, bloodhounds were used to track down escaped criminals. Nowadays, dogs are used more often to sniff out hidden caches of drugs such as heroin and marijuana.

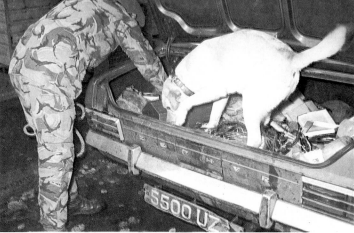

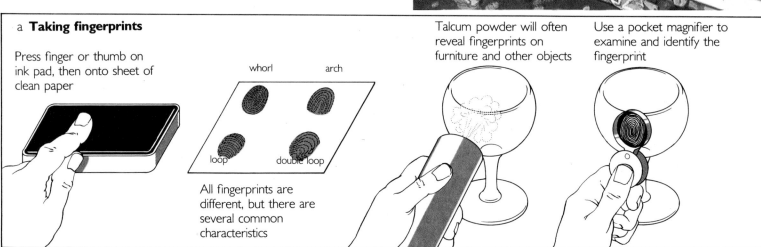

a **Taking fingerprints**

Press finger or thumb on ink pad, then onto sheet of clean paper

whorl   arch

loop   double loop

All fingerprints are different, but there are several common characteristics

Talcum powder will often reveal fingerprints on furniture and other objects

Use a pocket magnifier to examine and identify the fingerprint

Detective work calls for a combination of talents. A good detective has to be quick-witted and a fair psychologist who can guess what is going on in the minds of others, particularly the crook he is trying to track down. It also helps the detective if he has some scientific knowledge and training – because many criminals are also getting a better education these days! The use of scientific tests in detective work is called forensic science.

b Make a photo-fit kit

1 Get the best artist in your group to make full face portrait drawings of you all, all to the same size. Glue the portraits on stiff card

2 Cut each portrait as shown and assemble 'photo-fits' from the three different sections

hair and forehead

eyes and ears

mouth and chin

c Making invisible ink

To make the ink, fill a small bottle with water and add a tiny quantity of cobalt chloride. To read a message written in invisible ink, hold the paper close to heat. Lemon juice, milk, epsom salts and white or spirit vinegar can be used, too.

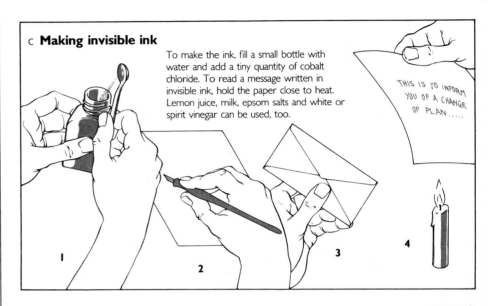

THIS IS TO INFORM YOU OF A CHANGE OF PLAN.....

1

2

3

4

d Match hairs and other evidence under your microscope

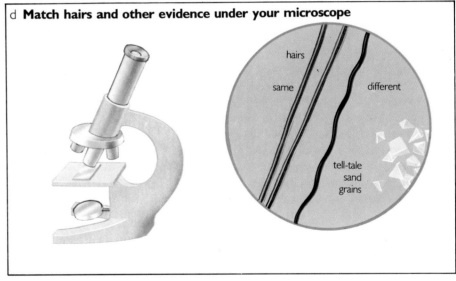

hairs

same

different

tell-tale sand grains

e Casting footprints

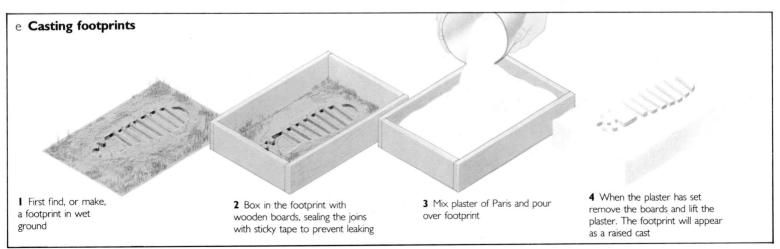

1 First find, or make, a footprint in wet ground

2 Box in the footprint with wooden boards, sealing the joins with sticky tape to prevent leaking

3 Mix plaster of Paris and pour over footprint

4 When the plaster has set remove the boards and lift the plaster. The footprint will appear as a raised cast

MAKE IT AND FLY IT

In legend, the first people to fly were the inventor Daedalus and his son Icarus, who wore bird-like wings attached to their arms with wax. But Icarus flew too near the Sun, and the wax melted...

In real life no-one flew until 1783, when two hot-air balloonists, the brothers Jacques and Joseph Montgolfier, and the hydrogen balloonist JAC Charles, all ascended skywards. Now flying is a regular part of modern life.

◀Ballooning for sport in Colorado, USA.

▲The earliest airplanes, at the beginning of our century, were often rather weird contraptions. Not all of them even got off the ground.

---

a Make a hot-air balloon

I m (39 in)

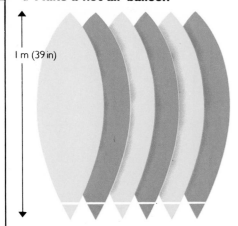

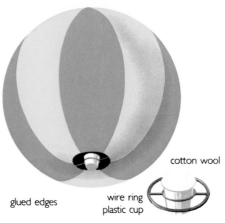

glued edges

cotton wool

wire ring
plastic cup

1 Cut 6 panels I m (39 in) long from uncreased pieces of tissue paper. Cut 5 cm (2 in) off one end of each panel. Glue panel edges together to form a balloon

2 Make a wire ring the same size as the hole. Put a plastic cup, eg a yogurt carton, in the central ring and fill with methylated spirits or wood alcohol and cotton wool. Glue open panel ends to wire ring.

3 Choose a calm, windless day to fly your balloon. Hold the balloon upright and partly expanded. Carefully light the cotton wool, watch the balloon expand....

...and away it goes

b Make a parachute

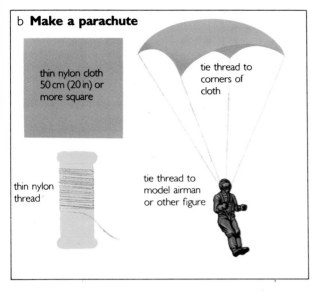

thin nylon cloth 50 cm (20 in) or more square

thin nylon thread

tie thread to corners of cloth

tie thread to model airman or other figure

▲By contrast with the early airplane (**opposite**), this albatross is a perfect 'flying machine'. It can sail in the skies for days on end, moving only the tips of its long, narrow wings.

c Make a paper glider

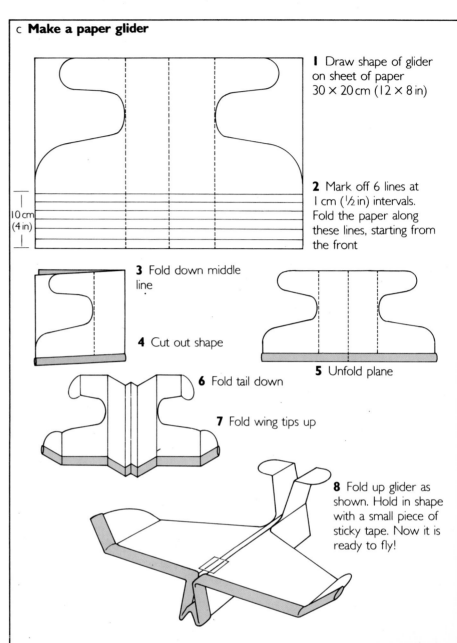

1 Draw shape of glider on sheet of paper 30 × 20 cm (12 × 8 in)

10 cm (4 in)

2 Mark off 6 lines at 1 cm (½ in) intervals. Fold the paper along these lines, starting from the front

3 Fold down middle line

4 Cut out shape

5 Unfold plane

6 Fold tail down

7 Fold wing tips up

8 Fold up glider as shown. Hold in shape with a small piece of sticky tape. Now it is ready to fly!

◄The General Dynamics F16 is a modern US jet fighter plane. It can travel at speeds exceeding Mach 2, or more than 2,390 kilometres per hour (1,520 miles per hour).

MAKE WINE
AND CIDER

▲The 'Mother of wine' – the juicy grapes of warmer lands. But in fact, wine can be made from almost any kind of fruit.

▲White burgundy is a type of wine that is often stored and matured in oak barrels.

◄A vineyard in the Côte d'Or region of France, where some of the best Burgundy wines come from.

The ancient Greeks made wine – and enjoyed drinking it. Since then, at least, wine has been one of the tastiest joys of life – taken, of course, in moderation! A glass of wine improves even the best of meals. Too much wine, like too much cider or any other alcoholic drink, can damage your health. Making wine and cider is great fun. The main thing to avoid is contamination by foreign microbes – so keep everything absolutely clean. The rest is just a matter of practice.

►If the grape is the mother of wine, then yeast is its genius. Yeast is a microscopic fungus – seen here magnified many thousands of times. Millions of yeast cells grow in each litre of fermenting wine, converting its sugar into alcohol. When all or most of the sugar has disappeared, the yeast is removed and the wine allowed to mature, often for several years, to improve its taste.

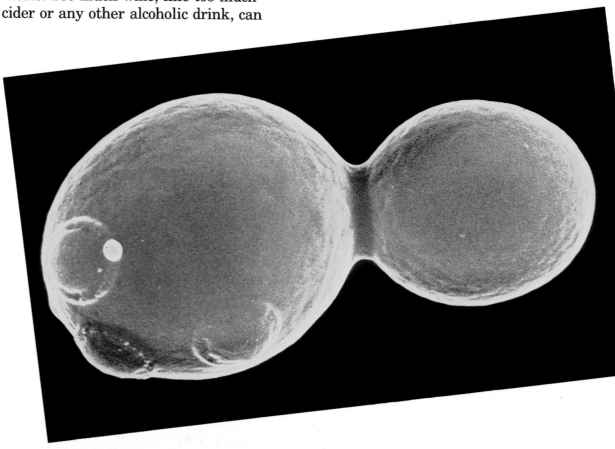

What you need

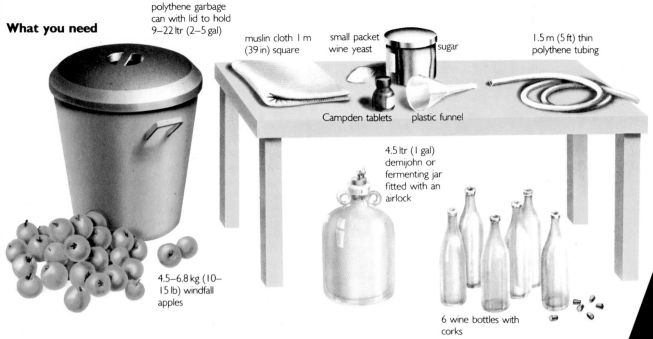

polythene garbage can with lid to hold 9–22 ltr (2–5 gal)

muslin cloth 1 m (39 in) square

small packet wine yeast

sugar

1.5 m (5 ft) thin polythene tubing

Campden tablets

plastic funnel

4.5 ltr (1 gal) demijohn or fermenting jar fitted with an airlock

4.5–6.8 kg (10–15 lb) windfall apples

6 wine bottles with corks

a To make apple wine

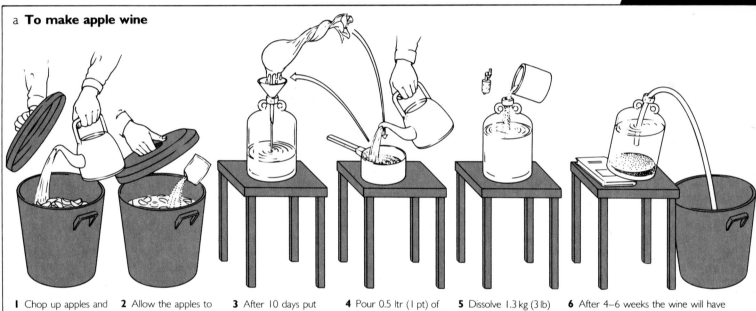

1 Chop up apples and put in bin. Pour not more than 2.25 ltr (½ gal) of boiling water over the apples

2 Allow the apples to cool to hand-warm. Add yeast, then put on lid. Rotate or shake for 5 minutes every day for 10 days

3 After 10 days put apple pulp into muslin square and squeeze juice through the muslin into the funnel in the neck of the demijohn

4 Pour 0.5 ltr (1 pt) of boiling water over squeezed apple mash to extract last juice. Add to contents of demijohn

5 Dissolve 1.3 kg (3 lb) of sugar in demijohn, make up with water to 3.3 ltr (¾ gal). Add airlock

6 After 4–6 weeks the wine will have fermented and the solids settled out. Siphon wine off. Pour siphoned wine back into cleaned demijohn. Repeat this operation as more solids settle out until the wine is clear. Then bottle the wine, adding ½ Campden tablet to each bottle. Leave for 3 months

b Making cider is even easier!

1 Chop the apples, put in the bin and crush them with a clean, heavy piece of wood

2 Remove pulp from bin, place on muslin and squeeze juice back into bin. Even better is to squeeze the pulp-filled cloth through an old-fashioned mangle

3 Add yeast. Put on lid. Leave for 4 days in a warm place

4 When frothing stops, pour cider into demijohn to complete fermentation

5 Drink after about 6 weeks

4 LOOKING AT NATURE

HOW PLANTS GROW

◀Bracken is a fern often found covering hillsides in temperate countries. Its feathery leaves or *fronds* (**left**) spring from an underground stem, or *rhizome*. When young the fronds are tightly curled, like a bishop's crook, or crozier, before uncurling (**above**).

a Light and air tests

Germinate a bean as shown below. **1** To prove that plants need air germinate another bean, this time adding iron filings to the jar and putting on an airtight lid. The bean will germinate, but the shoot will wilt because it lacks oxygen and carbon dioxide: no air gets into the jar and the iron filings rust and remove oxygen from air already in the jar. **2** To show that plants need light, germinate another bean in the dark. It will germinate normally but the shoot lacks green chlorophyll and soon stops growing

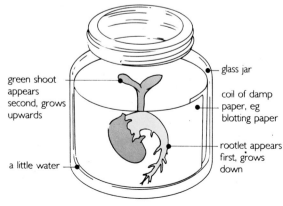

green shoot appears second, grows upwards

a little water

glass jar

coil of damp paper, eg blotting paper

rootlet appears first, grows down

b Make a leaf skeleton

Leaves and stems get their stiffness from many woody vessels, which also conduct water

around the plant, like tiny pipes. In leaves, these woody vessels form a fibrous skeleton which can be seen if you hold a leaf up to the light. But the leaf veins, or skeleton, can be revealed fully by cooking or digesting away all the rest of the leaf. To do this, first boil a fallen leaf or leaves in water together with a spoonful of washing soda, for about an hour. Then put the leaves in a strong solution of household bleach overnight. In the morning, everything except the skeleton of leaf veins will have floated away.

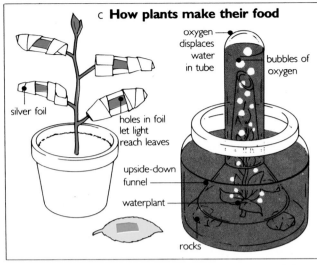

c How plants make their food

silver foil

holes in foil let light reach leaves

oxygen displaces water in tube

bubbles of oxygen

upside-down funnel

waterplant

rocks

Photosynthesis is the fundamental process by which green plants grow. The greenness of a plant is due to the pigment chlorophyll. When this pigment is exposed to sunlight, it helps turn the gas carbon dioxide, in the air inside the plant's leaves, into more complicated substances which build up the body of the plant as it grows. To show this, take a potted plant and place it in the dark for a few days, then wrap some of its leaves as shown, and put the plant in a bright light. After 3 hours, test the exposed leaf areas with a few drops of iodine solution. A blue color indicates starch — one of the complicated carbon compounds formed by photosynthesis. The covered areas will show no evidence of starch formation.

Photosynthesis also makes a plant give off oxygen. Test for this by trapping bubbles of oxygen, as they are given off, in a test tube as shown. Use a small underwater plant such as *Elodea*, the Canadian pondweed you can buy from any pet shop that sells things for fish or aquaria.

◄Plants will bend to face the light. This movement is not caused by muscle action, as in animals, but by growth. Cells in the plant stem on the side away from the light grow faster than those on the lit-up side, so causing the stem to bend towards the light.

▼A sequence of photographs showing the development and flowering of a hyacinth plant. These attractive plants are easy to grow in bowls indoors, in a window box or in the garden.

PROPAGATE YOUR PLANTS

▲A fine show of house plants. Clockwise from the red flowering begonia, they are: umbrella grass; a large, glossy-leaved philodendron; a cactus; an aloe; *Crassula*, a succulent with water-storing leaves; another cactus, and a yellow-leaved croton.

'*Propagate*' means 'to cause to reproduce and multiply'. If you have bought any indoor plants to brighten up your home, then most likely you will be able to propagate these, using fairly simple techniques as shown in the pictures. Home propagation will, of course, save you money, as well as being great fun. Some plants, such as busy lizzies, are so easy to propagate that in a summer or two you can fill a room with their bright flowers. Other potted plants are trickier to propagate or, like the philodendron in the photograph, grow so large that you may have room for only one of them.

a Succulents

(*Crassula* – money plant) is a good one to start with. Gently pull off a leaf and pot it directly, and water

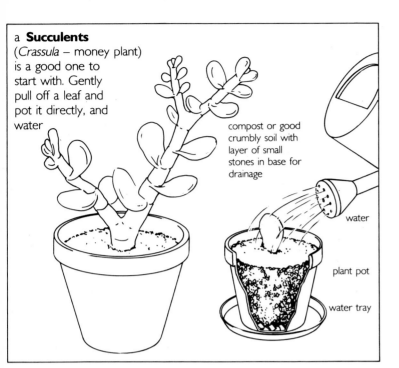

compost or good crumbly soil with layer of small stones in base for drainage

water

plant pot

water tray

b Flowering begonia

Take cutting of stem or new green shoot, dip cut end in rooting powder, and pot and water

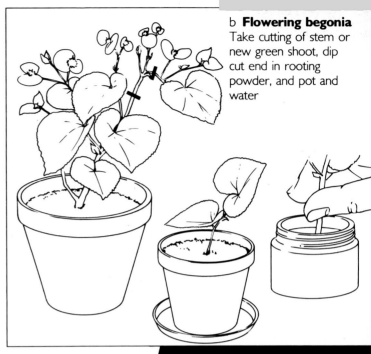

c Spider plant

(*Chlorophytum*) Break off a plantlet, pot directly, then water

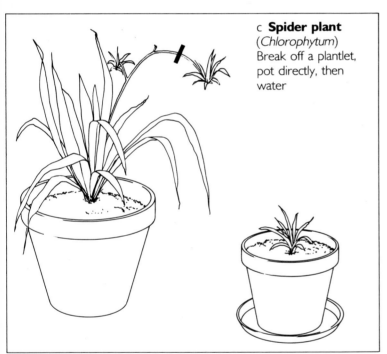

d Busy Lizzie

(*Impatiens*) Take a stem cutting with a few leaves. Put in water as shown. Pot when cutting has grown roots, and water

e Leafy begonia

(eg *Begonia rex*) Cut off a leaf by the stem. Lay it upside down and cut into sections with a sharp knife. Each section must have a bit of main vein. Pot in sharp sand over compost with the edge originally nearest the main stem downwards. Water

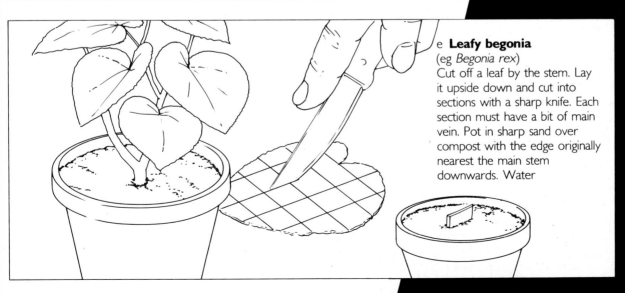

BUILD A POND

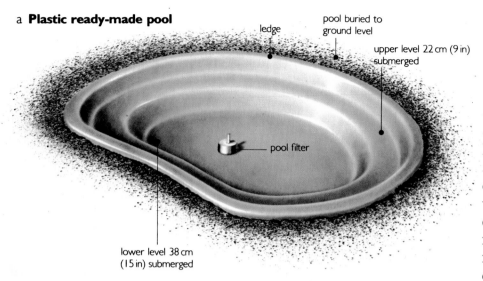

ledge

pool buried to ground level

upper level 22 cm (9 in) submerged

pool filter

lower level 38 cm (15 in) submerged

Gardeners are keen on ponds because they add to a garden's decorative attractions. But ponds are not only for gardeners. For anyone interested in natural history or biology (gardeners, of course, included) a garden pond is essential. The main reason is very simple. Ponds contain a greater variety of life in a small space than any other environment or living place. Though tremendously varied, this pond life is mostly small or even microscopic in size, so that a magnifying glass and, if possible, a microscope, should be part of your equipment.

b **Plastic-liner pool with three submerged levels** (cross section)

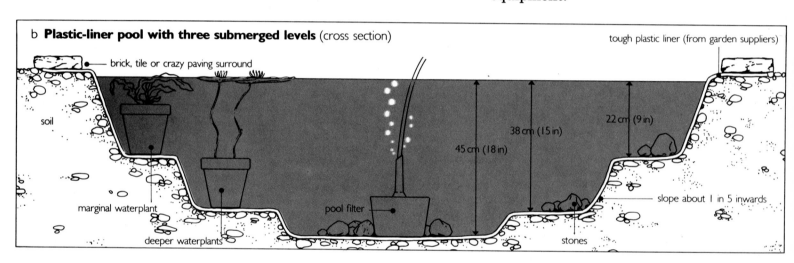

tough plastic liner (from garden suppliers)

brick, tile or crazy paving surround

soil

22 cm (9 in)

38 cm (15 in)

45 cm (18 in)

slope about 1 in 5 inwards

marginal waterplant

deeper waterplants

pool filter

stones

c **Digging the pool**

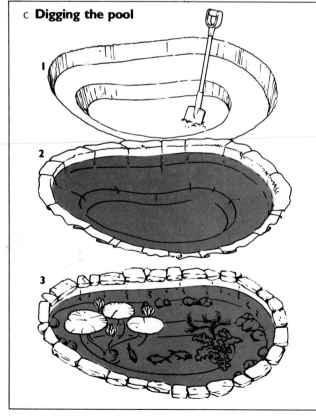

1 Dig the pool in an area of your garden that gets at least a half-day of sunlight
2 Line the pool. The area of plastic liner needed is: length + twice maximum width × width + twice maximum depth. So, if the pool is 1.8 m (6 ft) long and 1.5 m (5 ft) wide, the area of plastic is 1.8 m + 90 cm (6 ft + 3 ft) × 1.5 m + 90 cm (5 ft + 3 ft) or 2.7 m × 2.4 m (9 ft × 8 ft). Fill the pool with water, then peg liner into soil with 10 cm (4 in) nails
3 Lay a strong surround to protect the pool edge. Stock pool with plants and fish – other creatures will soon follow!

d **Make your own pool filter**

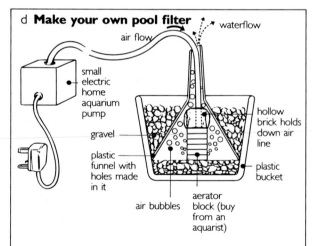

waterflow

air flow

small electric home aquarium pump

gravel

plastic funnel with holes made in it

air bubbles

aerator block (buy from an aquarist)

hollow brick holds down air line

plastic bucket

Any pool with an area less than 3.7 sq m (40 sq ft) will need a filter if it is not to choke up with slimy algae and smelly bacteria. Filters need not be expensive. This one aerates the water and also makes it circulate through the gravel, so filtering out dead and decaying matter. You will need to clean the filter about once a month during the spring and summer when everything grows fast

◀Water lilies and other water plants will make a garden pond both nicer to look at, and more attractive to wild life.

▼The common toad, with its golden eyes, is a handsome and welcome visitor to any pond or garden.

▲One creature to avoid, if your pond contains small fish! The pincer-jaws of this water beetle *larva* are needle sharp, and through them the larva pumps a powerful digestive juice that dissolves the body contents of its victims. Both the larva and the beetle it turns into, the great diving beetle, *Dytiscus marginalis*, are among the most ferocious predators of small pond life.

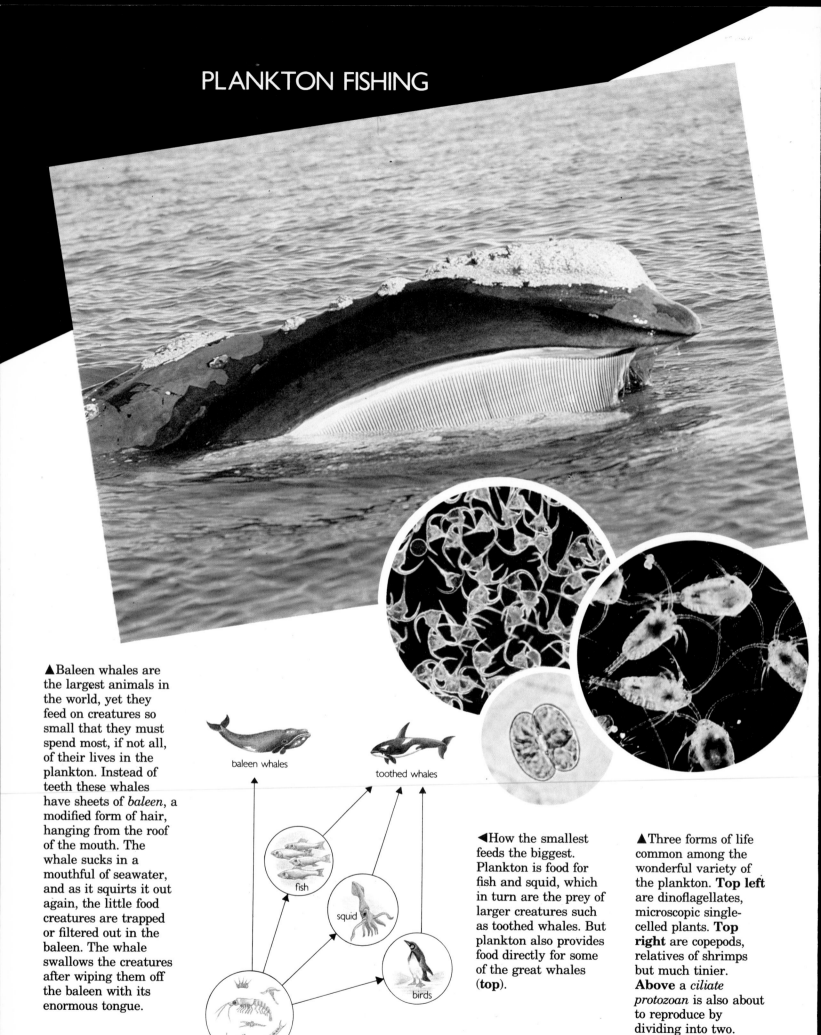

▲Baleen whales are the largest animals in the world, yet they feed on creatures so small that they must spend most, if not all, of their lives in the plankton. Instead of teeth these whales have sheets of *baleen*, a modified form of hair, hanging from the roof of the mouth. The whale sucks in a mouthful of seawater, and as it squirts it out again, the little food creatures are trapped or filtered out in the baleen. The whale swallows the creatures after wiping them off the baleen with its enormous tongue.

baleen whales

toothed whales

fish

squid

birds

plankton

◀How the smallest feeds the biggest. Plankton is food for fish and squid, which in turn are the prey of larger creatures such as toothed whales. But plankton also provides food directly for some of the great whales (**top**).

▲Three forms of life common among the wonderful variety of the plankton. **Top left** are dinoflagellates, microscopic single-celled plants. **Top right** are copepods, relatives of shrimps but much tinier. **Above** a *ciliate protozoan* is also about to reproduce by dividing into two.

Plankton is the mass of floating life in ponds, lakes, rivers and oceans. Most of the creatures and plants that make up the plankton are microscopic in size. They exist in huge numbers in the oceans' surface layers, where they provide food for many larger sea creatures. Phytoplankton, as microscopic floating plant-life is called, is in fact the main food-producer of the oceans, just as the grasses are in the world's land areas. Even a large pond or small lake can have plankton of great variety, as you can discover by fishing it with a plankton net.

a **Making a plankton net**

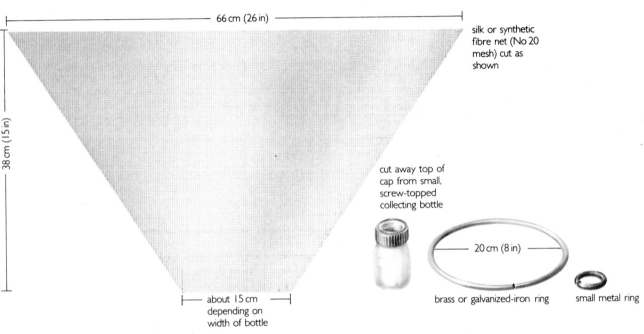

66 cm (26 in)

38 cm (15 in)

silk or synthetic fibre net (No 20 mesh) cut as shown

cut away top of cap from small, screw-topped collecting bottle

20 cm (8 in)

brass or galvanized-iron ring

small metal ring

about 15 cm depending on width of bottle

b **assembling the net**

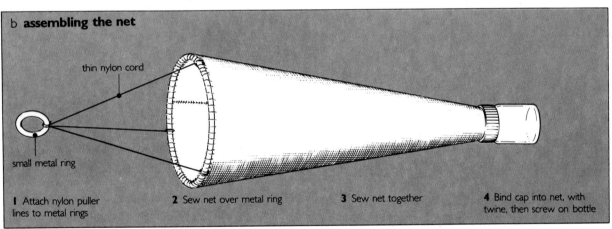

thin nylon cord

small metal ring

1 Attach nylon puller lines to metal rings

2 Sew net over metal ring

3 Sew net together

4 Bind cap into net, with twine, then screw on bottle

c **Using the net from a boat**

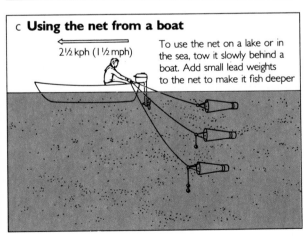

2½ kph (1½ mph)

To use the net on a lake or in the sea, tow it slowly behind a boat. Add small lead weights to the net to make it fish deeper

d **Using the net from the shore**

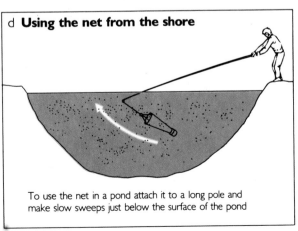

To use the net in a pond attach it to a long pole and make slow sweeps just below the surface of the pond

KEEPING PETS

People have kept pets for almost as long as people have been around. Dogs, for example, are descended from wolf- and jackal-like creatures that followed the earliest people around to feed from the food scraps they left behind. Eventually, these followers were adopted by the human groups as hunting and guard animals and simply as pets. Today we keep pets of all kinds, but there is only one main rule: Look after your pet! This means regular and suitable feeding, cleaning and attention from the vet when necessary. It also means *never* going away without arranging for someone to look after your pet or pets.

►Always good to look at, a cat is the most graceful of pets. These Burmese cats, though, are pedigree animals that would cost you a great deal! A further recommendation for the cat as a pet, is that it requires very little toilet training as a kitten.

Another advantage of cats as pets is that they don't need exercising as dogs do. This is an important consideration if you live in a city.

►Hamsters are among the most amusing of small pets, always entertainingly busy, when not asleep.

►Champions on show. Dogs, unlike cats, are pack animals, so that a dog, once used to the person who owns it, will afterwards show that person all the respect and faithfulness due to a senior member of the pack – if the dog is well trained and well treated, of course!

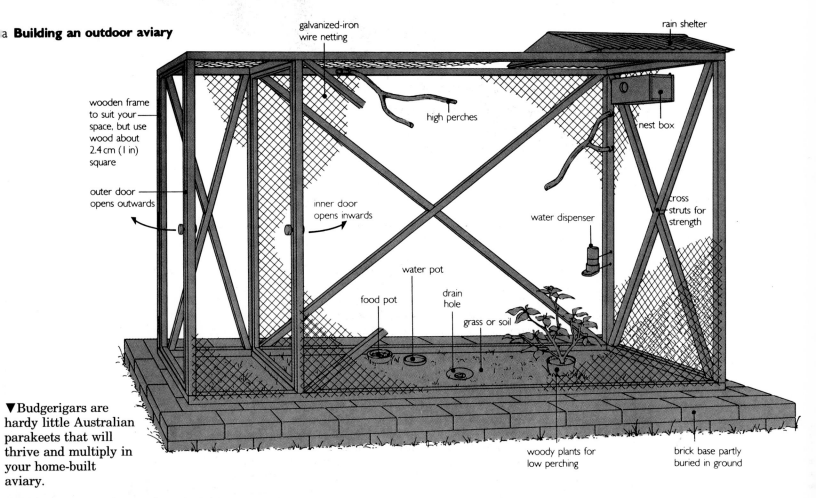

a **Building an outdoor aviary**

galvanized-iron wire netting

rain shelter

wooden frame to suit your space, but use wood about 2.4 cm (1 in) square

high perches

nest box

outer door opens outwards

inner door opens inwards

cross struts for strength

water dispenser

water pot

food pot

drain hole

grass or soil

▼Budgerigars are hardy little Australian parakeets that will thrive and multiply in your home-built aviary.

woody plants for low perching

brick base partly buried in ground

57

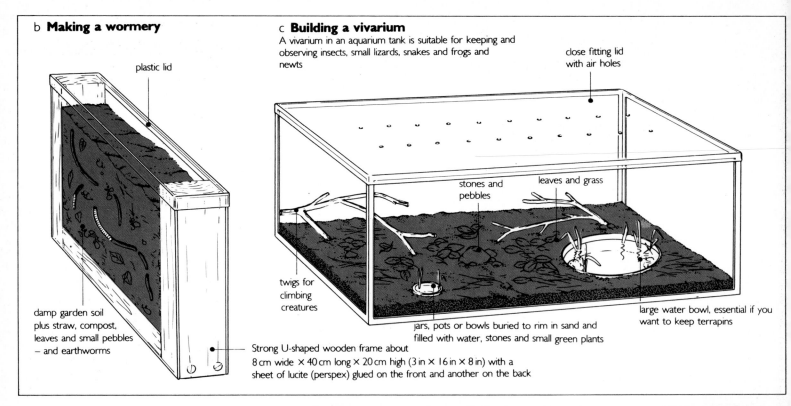

b Making a wormery

plastic lid

damp garden soil plus straw, compost, leaves and small pebbles – and earthworms

Strong U-shaped wooden frame about 8 cm wide × 40 cm long × 20 cm high (3 in × 16 in × 8 in) with a sheet of lucite (perspex) glued on the front and another on the back

c Building a vivarium

A vivarium in an aquarium tank is suitable for keeping and observing insects, small lizards, snakes and frogs and newts

close fitting lid with air holes

stones and pebbles

leaves and grass

twigs for climbing creatures

jars, pots or bowls buried to rim in sand and filled with water, stones and small green plants

large water bowl, essential if you want to keep terrapins

►This 3-horned chameleon from Africa is, in fact, a lizard. Chameleons are often kept as pets in Africa, because they are useful for keeping insects down in the house. The chameleon catches insects by shooting out its sticky tongue which is almost the length of its body. Apart from this lightning-fast movement, the chameleon usually moves at a very slow pace.

◄Larger than a pet mouse, this male Hercules beetle fills the palm of a boy's hand. By contrast, some beetles are the smallest of all insects, being no larger than the full stops on this page – and so quite useless as pets.

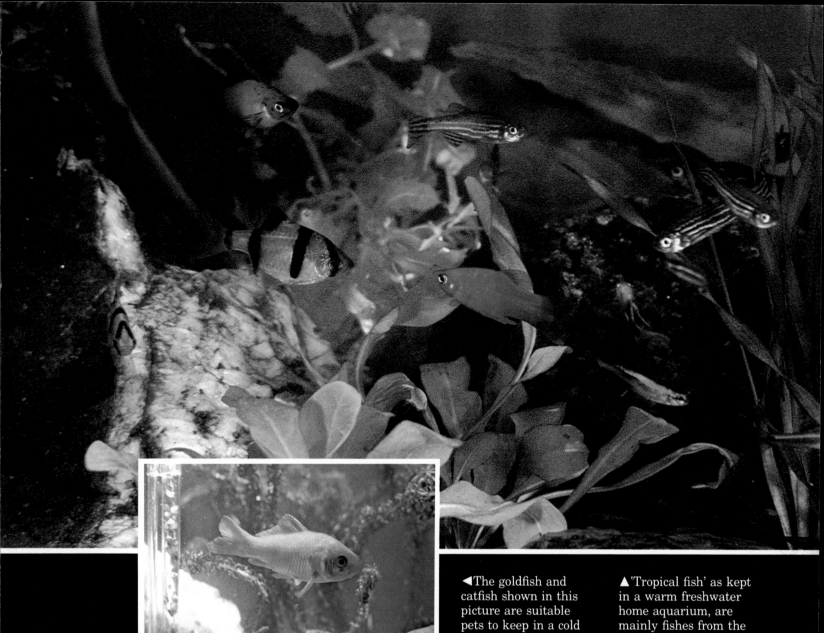

◄The goldfish and catfish shown in this picture are suitable pets to keep in a cold freshwater aquarium.

▲ 'Tropical fish' as kept in a warm freshwater home aquarium, are mainly fishes from the rivers of Central and South America, Africa and South-east Asia.

d **Establishing a home aquarium**

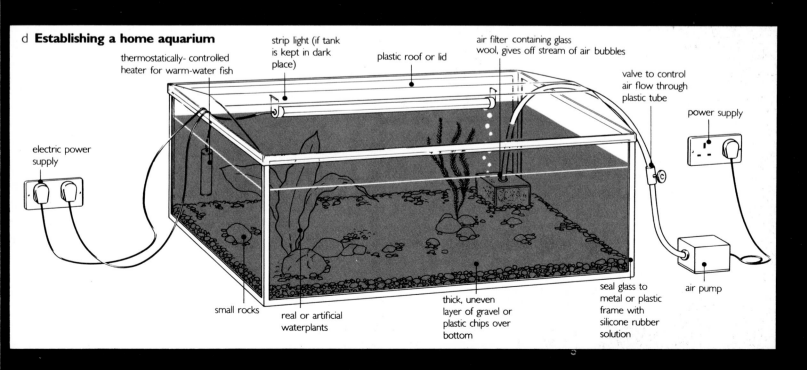

thermostatically- controlled heater for warm-water fish

strip light (if tank is kept in dark place)

plastic roof or lid

air filter containing glass wool, gives off stream of air bubbles

valve to control air flow through plastic tube

power supply

electric power supply

small rocks

real or artificial waterplants

thick, uneven layer of gravel or plastic chips over bottom

seal glass to metal or plastic frame with silicone rubber solution

air pump

KEEP AN ECOLOGY NOTEBOOK

Ecology is the study of animals, plants and other living creatures in their natural *habitats*, the places and conditions in which they live, feed and multiply. To know much about any living creature, even a pet animal, you have to know something about its natural environment. A pet bird, for example, may eat only seeds of a certain small size, which tells you that its natural environment or habitat is grassland, where such seeds are to be found. An ecology notebook will be easy enough to fill up, even from what you can observe by a close look at your garden or local park.

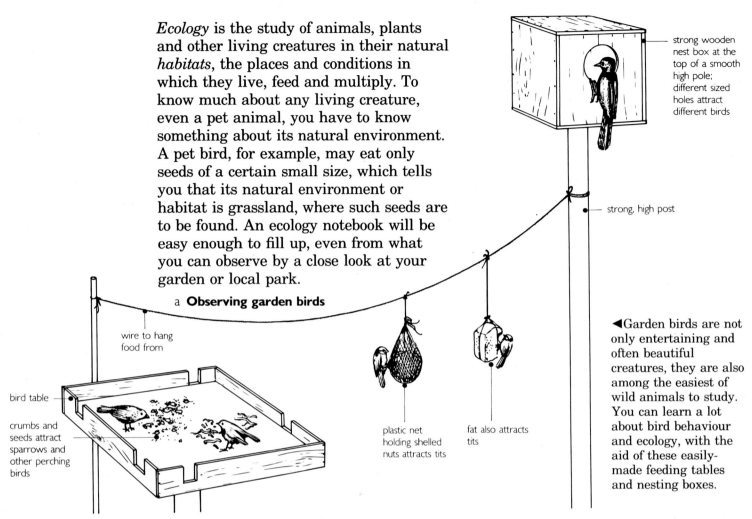

a Observing garden birds

strong wooden nest box at the top of a smooth high pole; different sized holes attract different birds

strong, high post

wire to hang food from

bird table

crumbs and seeds attract sparrows and other perching birds

plastic net holding shelled nuts attracts tits

fat also attracts tits

◄Garden birds are not only entertaining and often beautiful creatures, they are also among the easiest of wild animals to study. You can learn a lot about bird behaviour and ecology, with the aid of these easily-made feeding tables and nesting boxes.

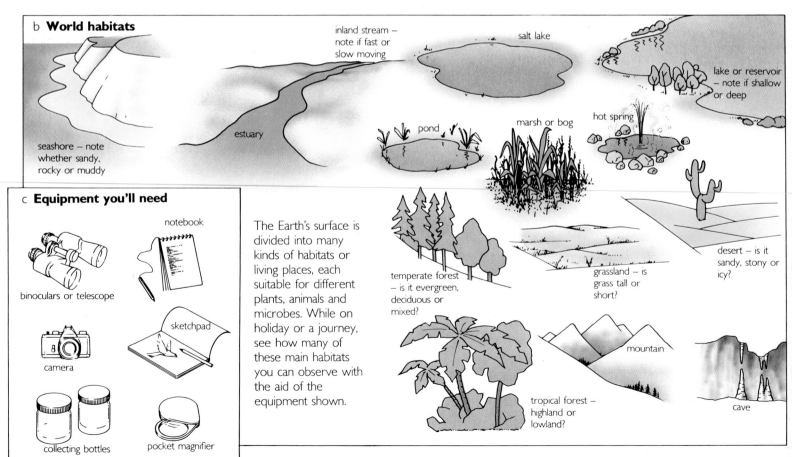

b World habitats

inland stream – note if fast or slow moving

salt lake

lake or reservoir – note if shallow or deep

estuary

pond

marsh or bog

hot spring

seashore – note whether sandy, rocky or muddy

c Equipment you'll need

notebook

binoculars or telescope

camera

sketchpad

collecting bottles

pocket magnifier

The Earth's surface is divided into many kinds of habitats or living places, each suitable for different plants, animals and microbes. While on holiday or a journey, see how many of these main habitats you can observe with the aid of the equipment shown.

temperate forest – is it evergreen, deciduous or mixed?

grassland – is grass tall or short?

desert – is it sandy, stony or icy?

tropical forest – highland or lowland?

mountain

cave

d **Mini-habitats**

tree canopy

house eaves and gutters

wooden fence

rotten wood

house drain

leaf litter

lawn

dead grass or straw

pond

holes in old bricks or plaster

table plot – turned earth

bushes and flowerbeds

◄Gardens and parks are places rich in life, with many habitats. Observe and record all the small plants and creatures you can find, together with notes on where you find them. A magnifying glass will again be useful.

Bird-spotting is a popular hobby for many people interested in natural history. Even with binoculars, a bird is often best recognized by its silhouetted shape as it flies, perches or feeds.

e **Populations**

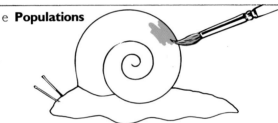

Estimate the number of snails in your garden by harmlessly spot-marking 10 with a dab of brown paint on the shell. Release them at different places in the garden.

A week later catch another batch of snails. A group of 12 may contain 2 marked ones.

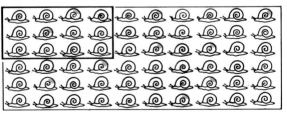

The group of 12 contains 2 out of 10, or $\frac{1}{5}$ of the marked snails. So the total snail population will be about $5 \times 12 = 60$. Remember that the number can only be approximate because snails do not mix evenly and birds may have eaten some. In general:

$$\frac{\text{total}}{\text{population}} = \frac{\text{total number marked}}{\text{number marked in sample group}} \times \frac{\text{total number in}}{\text{sample group}}$$

seagull

swift

barn owl

condor

swallow

American woodpecker

golden eagle

robin

wren

white stork

turkey

mallard duck

GLOSSARY

Alloy Hard substance made up of one or more kinds of metal, with perhaps some other, non-metallic, substances as well. Steel, brass and aluminum are three examples of alloys.

Atom The smallest part of a chemical element that still has all the properties of that element. For example, a single atom of the gas hydrogen will still have all the properties of that gas, but anything smaller will not.

Baleen A modified type of hair which hangs in sheets from the roofs of the mouth of some types of whale. These whales eat plankton and use the sheets of baleen as a sort of sieve to strain the plankton from the sea water.

Bedding plane The direction in which a rock splits most easily.

Binocular vision The ability, such as humans have, for both eyes to focus on the same object so enabling things to be seen in depth.

Chemistry Study of the composition of substances (how they are made up of simpler substances) and of their effects on one another in chemical reactions.

Ciliate Microscopic organism that has minute hair-like threads, or cilia, projecting from the surface of its body. The beating of the cilia helps the organism to move through the water in which it lives.

Devonian Geological period that lasted from about 410 to 345 million years ago.

Ecology The study of the way in which living things interrelate with each other and their surroundings.

Electron A sub-atomic particle – that is, something smaller than an atom – which has a negative electric charge.

ESP (Extra-sensory perception) Knowledge acquired in a way that does not use the ordinary senses. Trying to 'read' someone's mind by telepathy is an example of attempting to use extra-sensory perception. 'Extra' in this phrase means 'beyond' or 'outside'. This type of perception is not scientifically proven.

Fossils Remains of prehistoric organisms preserved in rocks.

Frond Leaflike part of some flowerless plants, such as ferns.

Geology The study of the Earth.

Gravity The force of attraction betwen all particles of matter in the Universe. Here on Earth we experience gravity mostly as the weight of substances, which is simply the force with which the Earth attracts these substances.

Habitat The natural home of any living organism.

Larva (plural **larvae**) A stage in the life cycle of an insect from the time it leaves the egg until it changes into the adult form.

Laser Device using intense light energy. The word laser comes from '*l*ight *a*mplification by *s*timulated *e*mission of *r*adiation'.

Lateral line sense The ability of fish to feel pressure waves under water. The cells sensitive to this pressure are located in a line along each side of the fish's body.

Mainframe A large computer. In general mainframe computers have very much larger memories and work much faster than home computers.

Mare The Latin word for 'sea'. In astronomy it is used to describe areas of depression on the surface of the Moon. The early astronomers, who first used the term, thought these areas were seas. Powerful modern telescopes and exploration of the Moon have shown that there is no water on its surface.

Mesopotamia An area of ancient civilization in south-western Asia between the Tigris and Euphrates rivers. Today, the country of Iraq covers much the same area.

Molecule A substance consisting of two or more atoms linked together.

Native metal A pure metal occurring naturally within the Earth. Gold, copper, silver and mercury may be found as native metals.

Photosynthesis The process by which plants make their own food and body

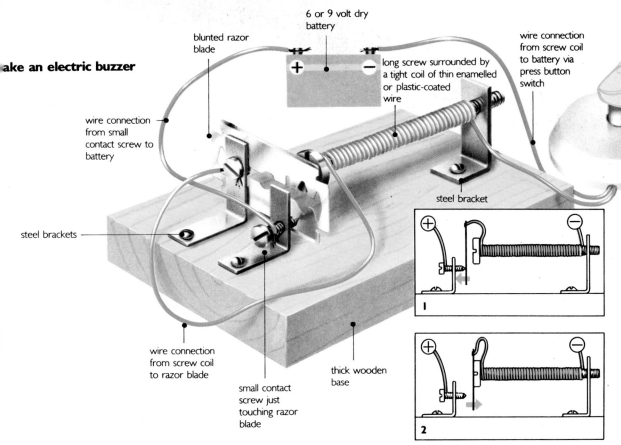

Make an electric buzzer

6 or 9 volt dry battery

blunted razor blade

long screw surrounded by a tight coil of thin enamelled or plastic-coated wire

wire connection from screw coil to battery via press button switch

wire connection from small contact screw to battery

press button switch (from electrical suppliers)

steel bracket

steel brackets

wire connection from screw coil to razor blade

small contact screw just touching razor blade

thick wooden base

How it works: When switch button is pressed the electrical circuit is completed and electricity flows through the wire from one pole of the battery to the other. The small contact screw, with its point touching the razor blade, is part of this circuit (**1**). As the electric current flows through the wire coiled around the long screw, the long screw becomes an electromagnet (page 28). The electromagnet then pulls the razor blade away from the contact screw (**2**). This breaks the circuit, no electricity flows through the coil, so the electromagnet is de-energized. The razor blade springs back, makes contact with the screw, energizes the electromagnet again – and so on. As the razor blade springs back and forth between the screws it makes a buzzing sound. The farther apart the screws, the louder the buzz.

substances from carbon dioxide in the air, water and sunlight.

Physics Scientific study of the composition and interaction of matter and energy.

Phytoplankton Plankton consisting of microscopic plants.

Plankton Minute plants and animals that live in vast numbers in water and are carried about by water movements, for example, currents and tides.

Propagate To cause to reproduce and multiply. Many different types of plant can be propagated by taking and growing cuttings from the parent plant.

Protozoan (plural **protozoa**) Single-celled animal, usually microscopic in size.

Refraction The bending of radiation when it passes from one medium to another of a different density, for example, light rays passing from water to air.

Relative density The amount by which one substance is heavier or lighter than another.

Rhizome A plant stem that grows horizontally along, or beneath, the surface of the ground, and produces both roots and shoots.

Specific gravity The specific gravity of any substance is the weight of the substance compared with the weight of the same volume of water. Thus aluminium is 2.7 times as heavy as water, so it has a specific gravity of 2.7.

Stalactite Icicle-like formation generally found hanging from the roof of a cave and formed from calcium carbonate deposited by water trickling through the cave's roof.

Stalagmite Like a stalactite, a deposit of calcium carbonate generally found in caves, but 'growing' up from the floor of the cave.

Tertiary Geological period that lasted from 64 to 2 million years ago.

Voltage Electrical force. It is measured in units called volts. An electric current, which is measured in amperes or amps, will flow through a wire more easily if there is a high voltage 'forcing' it through the wire.

INDEX

Acknowledgements
Archivio B, Chris Baker, M.Bertinetti, C.Bevilacqua, P.Brierly, Ron Boardman, Camera Press, Bruce Coleman, N.Cirani, R.J.Corbin, De Beers Industrial Diamond Division, Werner Forman, Michael Holford, IBM, Archivio Igda, Jacana, A.Margiocco, MARKA, Musee de l'Air, NASA, Nature Photographers, N.H.P.A., Photri, Picturepoint, G.Pozzoni, K.G.Preston, Colin Salmon, M.Savionius, Science Museum London, Science Photo Library, Seaphot, Spectrum, Frank Spooner Picture Syndication International, Titus, Victoria and Albert Museum, D.P.Wilson, ZEFA. Drawings and diagrams: Graham Rosewarne and Janos Marffy.